THE HAPPINESS QUEST

THE HAPPINESS
QUEST

Richard Yaxley

An Omnibus Book from Scholastic Australia

Omnibus Books
an imprint of Scholastic Australia Pty Ltd
(ABN 11 000 614 577)
PO Box 579, Gosford NSW 2250.
www.scholastic.com.au

Part of the Scholastic Group
Sydney • Auckland • New York • Toronto • London • Mexico City
• New Delhi • Hong Kong • Buenos Aires • Puerto Rico

First published by Scholastic in 2018.
Text copyright © Richard Yaxley, 2018.
Cover design copyright © Steve Wells, 2018.

A catalogue record for this
book is available from the
NATIONAL
LIBRARY   National Library of Australia
OF AUSTRALIA

ISBN 978 1 74299 199 3 (paperback)

Typeset in 11.5/17pt Caslon

Printed and bound by Griffin Press.
Scholastic Australia's policy, in association with Griffin Press, is to use papers
that are renewable and made efficiently from wood grown in responsibly
managed forests, so as to minimise its environmental footprint.

10 9 8 7 6 5 4 3 2 1   18 19 20 21 22 / 1

For the San Sisters, past and present.
Live joyfully!

We look so long at the closed door that we do not see the one which has been opened for us.

Helen Keller

PART

I

It was during one of those confusing days when the sun blazed in an overly bright sky yet the moon was still visible that Tillie Bassett first saw the Happiness Clinic.

Homework Club at school, Tillie trying valiantly to catch up on all that missed work and somehow shine a light on the ever-deepening darkness that was algebra, the tutor running overtime because there were so many students who, like Tillie, didn't see why polynomial solutions were vital, more so it seemed than those terrible floods in China or the war in Syria, war in Afghanistan, *wars* in Africa, and now her mother Susan was late for her six-weekly foils and trim, which was devastating because that prissy Samantha would move straight on to the next appointment, leaving Susan to wait, wait, wait, with nothing to do but be appalled by those androgynous-model magazines with their patronising ads for anti-ageing cream and anti-sag appliances; worst thing of all, Susan had left her phone at home, on charge.

'Sorry,' said Tillie. Again.

'Oh, it's not down to you.' Susan manoeuvred impatiently into a side street to avoid yet more roadworks then clicked her tongue as an amber light dared to turn red. 'Sometimes the universe just conspires.'

They stopped behind a decrepit-looking ute, Tillie gazing forlornly at her knees, which seemed so dimpled these days, unattractive, even elderly, while her mother scanned the sky, the street, the immediate unhelpful world.

'Tillie,' she said eventually.

'Sorry –'

'No, look. Over there.'

Tillie saw it immediately. The Happiness Clinic provided a footnote to a group of small box-buildings clumped in a style that crooned smugly, *we're not quite linear but we sure are pretending*. Each box had a pragmatic label over the door: *Feet, Teeth, Eyes, Bones, Skin, Blood … Happiness?* The biggest area seemed to be reserved for *Skin*, but the entire building, painted the colour of sunflower petals, looked holistic as if, thought Tillie, a person could weave her way through while being checked, injected, recalibrated, mended, cleansed and purified. Total makeover; welcome to the Wonderful New You.

'The one at the end,' said her mother.

'Yes.' Up ahead Tillie sensed the light turn green, the ute smoking its way forward.

'Want me to check it out?' asked Susan with more kindness than usual.

To appease her mother Tillie murmured okay, thank you – but it was hard not to stare at her old-woman knees, harder still not to dissolve into a wet, tissuey mess as they sidestepped the afternoon traffic and drove silently into the silver heat of the city.

She couldn't remember a specific moment: that was the worst thing. No flash or sinkhole. It had been two or three months ago, in the middle part of that overheated saucepan of a summer, when Tillie had found herself sitting for no reason, waiting for no one, thinking of nothing – and there it was.

Sadness. Deep, terrible, devastating.

After that, after she'd registered the feeling, named it, gauged some measure of its depth and size, Tillie had hoped that the sadness might troop away, disgruntled with being so swiftly exposed – but the stupid thing had done the opposite, decided to remain and pull Tillie into a dark space that might have had walls, might not, but was unyielding anyway, pushing her into the black.

Alone, afraid. Then accusations, hustling through the darkness –

You're worthless.

You're helpless.

It's all pointless.

Sad Tillie Bassett. Each word was a dart that hissed and hurt. Sad, stupid and scared. Why were you even born?

This deep, sudden tangle of uncertainty, whereas in the past – not so long ago, though it was rapidly seeming like an age – Tillie had regularly found herself basking comfortably, happily, in the white and luminous light, a place, she thought, where she was worthy and helpful and there *had* been a point to it all. Not always seeable, of course, but there nevertheless. A place where she was part of a simple, familiar system, where you were gifted a life and that life would evolve in patterns that were to be cherished and enjoyed. There was the core pattern, the unbreakable love of Family and Friends, then the pattern of School and probably University followed by a Good Career. Later on would come the pattern of partnership with That One Special Person, allowing other sub-patterns to evolve: her own family inside her own home, episodes of travel, industry and a general worthwhileness, the steady, satisfying gathering of experiences that spoke of a life well lived.

Now, for no obvious reason, the patterns had been blocked and broken … as if someone had snapped the end of a kaleidoscope and hurled all the coloured bits into space.

She'd been terrified of broadcasting. Telling someone. Even if she could, who? Her mother was often impatient. Her recently retired father was busy writing and rewriting The Book That Would Never Get Written. Her older sister Rosie was preoccupied with the farm that the rest of the family never visited and Niko, the Loveliest Fiancé in the World. Her best friend Macy was too glorious and bouncing to be saddled with the drag of Tillie's woe. Nor Snake, doe-eyed Snake with his ginger dreads – the guy was saintly. He'd been born to save the world, not her.

Eventually, her mother.

Susan Bassett was a part-time painter and full-time sculptor who used clay, cardboard, tin cans, rubber, milk cartons, cogs, screws and wires taken from old appliances – anything, as long as it was tactile. One Saturday morning she'd called Tillie into her downstairs studio and asked for her opinion. The metal shape was abstract, but Tillie immediately thought of a wingless bird tilting its narrow beak to the horizon, the golden future.

'Well?'

'Great.'

'Uh-huh.'

'Smooth,' said Tillie, knowing that her mother would want detail, in abundance. 'I like how it flows.'

'Flows,' repeated Susan. She stood back from the sculpture, interlocked her fingers, stared and thought and stared some more. Rubbed her fingers critically over a metal tip.

'Sweetie,' she said, 'what's wrong?'

Tillie flushed, her eyes filling quickly with hot tears. She felt her mother's hands on her upper arms, rubbing and kneading as if, thought Tillie, she wants to reshape me. Get some flow happening.

'There's something,' said Susan. 'Isn't there?'

Which was when Tillie had told her. I'm sad, she'd said, and I don't know why. I wake up sad, stay sad all day, go to bed sad. Mum, it's horrible. I live in a nice house, people are good to me, I get okay marks at school, I have things, whatever I want really, I'm totally, utterly privileged … Mum, she said, it's embarrassing because I'm so lucky compared to, you know, others and yet, yet, I can't help it –

'Sad,' said Susan, Tillie nodding, looking with wet eyes at the sculpture because that at least seemed solid and purposeful.

'About what, exactly?'

Living. Dying. Not knowing what might happen. Not knowing what had happened. Such big labels; she couldn't begin to explain.

Her mother waited a moment longer then asked, 'Was there something specific? Something at school? First few weeks of a new year, might take a while to adjust.'

'Nothing specific,' Tillie told her.

'Friends okay?'

'Yes.'

'Teachers?'

'Mum,' said Tillie, 'I don't know why. I wish I did but it's just, I'm just –' She bent her head and flexed her feet and felt a sudden, vicious hatred for the lump that she'd become. Perhaps, she thought, I could pull away the skin and gouge out all the blubber, then my mother could replace my body with clay or tin, anything tactile, and I could be put on display in a glass case and people could stare at me, the girl who became a statue –

That ancient myth, Pygmalion? No, other way around.

She felt her mother's arms again, surprisingly strong for someone of her diminutive stature.

'Time to see Doctor Ev,' said Susan firmly, and Tillie, although she didn't think there'd be much to be gained from doing so, agreed.

But first, Canondale College, known with varying degrees of affection as 'The Cannon', from which graduates were annually projected into the ever-grateful world, young women and men of extraordinary honesty, reliability, integrity …

Poetry with Ms Graham. Normally Tillie loved poetry and she loved Ms Graham, who was refreshingly nutty in a mismatched smock-and-trousers, giant-parrot-earrings kind of way. Ms Graham looked like a grown-up Rugrat.

Today, a poem about apples, about love.

> *I plucked pink blossoms from mine apple tree*
> *And wore them all that evening in my hair:*
> *Then in due season when I went to see*
> *I found no apples there.*

Simone Varela read the poem in a lilting voice that touched corners and hearts, Simone who was a lead in *Godspell* despite 'only' being in Year Ten, then Ms Graham graphically organised the whiteboard in her haphazard manner: the apple as a symbol, fruit of temptation, golden apples in the Garden of Hesperides; knowledge, immortality, sin.

And Tillie began to cry.

At first a sniffle, like an allergy, but very soon, tears. She tried to smother the gulps and carps, that breathy, horribly public statement of crying, impossible, particularly when Carmen and Billy either side of her were staring – but the worst part, the utter terror, was that she didn't know why she was doing this. Oh, God, she thought, if you the false and you're tuning in today, please tell me, why? When it was nothing more than an English class with Ms Graham, no different from usual, nothing more than a poem, beautiful, yes – 'Ah Willie, Willie, was my love less worth' – but just a poem; Tillie read them all the time, sometimes even wrote them! True, poems might make you think into unusual places and feel some bits and pieces that could be uncomfortable, but to sob like this, uncontrollable now, beyond –

'Tillie,' said Ms Graham. 'Tillie, love, come with me.'

She felt so stupid, trying to rise, weak in the legs, self-important Carmen sweeping up her books and laptop, no doubt hoping for a ringside seat – 'She was, like, totally out of it, such a zonk' – staggering through the door to the echoey corridor, Ms Graham half holding her as she tried to balance tenderness with the conventions of respect.

'Breathe,' she said urgently. 'Think of nothing else. Just breathe.'

Took a while but it worked, inasmuch that Tillie stopped sobbing, but now she felt depleted, as if gluttonous blood bugs had infiltrated and drained her. Ms Graham twisted the thick multi-coloured rings on her fingers and said, 'Tillie, do you need to go home?'

Don't know, she thought. Don't know anything –

'Carmen will take you to Transition.'

She sat opposite the counsellor – 'Call me Allegra' – who was ratlike, although a pretty rat. Odd that there could be such a thing, rats having a reputation as ugly and furtive disease-carriers, but Allegra's features were symmetrical and close to perfect. She also had extraordinarily vivid eyes and a habit of leading into a conversation with her nose.

'Tell me what happened,' she said. Afterthought, 'Take your time.'

'I lost it,' Tillie told her.

'You were upset?'

Well, obviously. Not exactly boundless tears of joy –

'Yes.'

'Because?'

Tillie shrugged. 'Don't know.'

'Matilda –'

'Tillie.'

'Sorry. Tillie, there must have been a reason.'

No, she thought. Not really. A brief flash of indignation; why must there be a reason? Why must everything be – that word, science word – why must everything be *causal*? Can't some things just happen of their own accord? Zap, here I am. Zup, there I go.

She said, 'Miss, I'm okay now –'

'Tillie,' said Allegra patiently, 'you had a meltdown and we need to find out why. Look,' – she held up a picture card – 'flowers don't simply appear. They come from a plant, which comes from a seed.'

'Yes, Miss.'

Another picture card. 'A storm,' said Allegra, 'occurs because of the collision of moisture and warm air.' Nose out, leaning in. 'And crying, sobbing, occurs because we're upset, and we become upset because something has happened in our lives to make us that way.'

We?

Allegra said, 'It's your choice, of course, always your choice, but in my experience the best way to deal with a problem is to share it.'

Wish I could, thought Tillie. Wish it was *causal*. Wish I

could say, okay, Miss, this is how it was … had a bad dream, my friend dumped me, my mother called me a leech, my father didn't recognise me at breakfast. None of those was desirable, of course, but at least they'd explain … No.

No bad dream because I didn't sleep. In fact, last night there was nothing in my head except black, and it was grainy. Like sand or ash, relentlessly filling every space.

Macy and Snake, still friends.

At breakfast Mum took time out from burning the cheese omelette to hug me and call me capital-G gorgeous. Dad said hey-ho tiger and suggested a movie sometime soon, just us, kiddo, maybe the Italian film festival. Yay, Tuscany and tomatoes.

Share it? Can't. Nothing to share.

She shook her head. 'Sorry, Miss.'

A bit more to-ing and fro-ing until eventually Allegra had satisfied herself by providing Tillie with another appointment, giving her pencils and a colouring-in book – really? – and carefully placing her in the Transition lounge: beanbags and pastel walls, a basket of soft toys, Handel and candles. Tillie chose the palest beanbag and sat obediently. She was tired from the night, the chaotic morning, the denseness of it all. In the past, she thought, there'd been other moments – minutes, hours, days even when she'd been sad … of course there had. Everyone was sad from time to time. But those instances had definitely stemmed from an event, like Mister Chirp, her beloved canary, pale and stiff on the newspaper one morning. At the age of eight she'd been devastated, a hole bored into her satin self, but she'd learned to cope with that, the hole still there but part of her now. Everyone's identity had holes. Some closed, some were patched, some just stayed and you learned to avoid them.

No biggie there.

Likewise, the death of her grandma – Henry's mother – whom she'd never really known beyond those occasional, sputtering phone calls to and from Melbourne. That was another sadness come from death, but more so, for Tillie, the loss of that future occasion when she and her grandma might have come to know each other. Realising that you wouldn't have the chance to properly know and love those whom you should was very sad – but still a hole, and holes can be dealt with.

Another time, the Most Terrible Time, when she was very young and her mother had screeched her pain and fled to Luana's place. Daddy, who's Luana? A friend, apparently, from long ago. Trusted. Henry had said desperately, 'She needs a break, that's all, a break!' but Tillie had known otherwise, because fourteen-year-old Rosie had told her. 'They're arguing,' she'd said. 'I hear them. They think I'm asleep but I'm not. I'm awake and I hear them saying bad stuff.'

Fear, like a cold wind skimming Tillie's skin as Rosie traced a fingertip up and down the length of her own facial scar, an automated response to change.

'Want to know what they said?'

No!

'Yes.'

'Dad said, don't go back there, and Mum said, what if I can't help it? Then she said, hopeless, it's hopeless, there's no future.'

Whereupon little Tillie had asked, 'What's a fut-ure?' but Rosie hadn't answered, instead beating her hands without rhythm upon her bedhead and saying, 'Maybe that's us. No future with us. Maybe it's over? Maybe she won't come back?' Rosie had smiled and sung, but for Tillie the thought of a motherless landscape was a profound sadness, and another kind of death ... However, Susan did return, the vacuum gradually filled with whispers that grew to chatter, the angry shapes in Susan's studio became more flowing, and soon enough she, Tillie, was basking in renewed love. The aftermath of that Most Terrible Time had been like an orchard, fresh apples and morning showers.

One more of note, when Snake's newborn brother had died. Poor baby had been just three days old but with a heart too unformed for the life that it needed to support. Tillie had been sad for Jackson, sad for the family, but saddest for Snake, her friend bleached and hollow like a poured-out milk container. She'd never forgotten the day he visited, bringing a jigsaw. The image was a painting – Van Gogh, said her father, wandering by, touching Snake tenderly on the crown – with a road and a cypress tree. They'd sat at the kitchen table and placed the pieces until there was one to go.

Tillie had said, 'You finish,' but Snake, holding the piece tightly, had refused to do so, eventually dropping it back in the box and dismantling the rest of the jigsaw.

The bell rang, muted in Transition. Tillie placed the pencils and book neatly on a shelf. She thought of the final line of the love-and-apples poem – *I loitered, while the dews fell fast I loitered still* – and she remembered Snake sitting at the table, shuddering as if mechanised. She hadn't known what to do, her own misery seeming so second-hand. Eventually Snake had scooped all of the pieces into the box. He'd thanked her politely, left the house and they'd not spoken of Jackson since.

Dr Ev had been the Bassett family doctor since the original, Dr Barnabas, had gone to Italy to visit an ailing relative and not returned.

'Lost to antiquity,' Tillie's father had mused.

'Lost to the pizza parlour, more like,' her mother had retorted, Dr Barnabas having been a very large man with very large lolly packs in his top drawer, whereas Dr Ev was a low-charging bullock, round-shouldered, rust-coloured. She was a good doctor – thorough, matter-of-fact, knew most things about the world – and always friendly, but Tillie was still in awe of her. Announcements of problem and cure were weighted heavily as if the doctor were – another word, from religion classes – as if she were *omniscient*. And *omnipotent*. The God-words, fair enough because Dr Ev was a god. She'd be comfortable with a quiver full of lightning bolts, thought Tillie, and a magic staff. Maybe even a beard.

'Well,' said the doctor, puffing a little as she extricated herself from a swivel chair, 'sometimes life can be inconsiderate. Let's see.' She checked Tillie's blood pressure, listened to her heart, measured her, weighed her, looked into her throat, ears and eyes, pushed strong fingers into her abdomen then said, 'Nothing you know of that's bothering you?'

'No.'

'Feeling a bit overwhelmed?'

'I guess. Not really.'

'Which one, Tillie?'

'I don't feel overwhelmed,' Tillie told her truthfully. 'I feel sad.'

'Can be the same thing. Feels like sad when it's actually a state of compression. You're compressed because everything is coming at you, hard. All those expectations, from home, school, friends, boyfriend –'

'I don't have a boyfriend.'

'Good girl. Stick with that. You see what I'm saying, though? Compression, which leads to anxiety –'

'No,' said Tillie, 'I don't – it's not that. I'm sorry, I'm not very good at describing. I just feel –'

If she could draw a picture, she thought, it would be black. And empty. And noisy. And grainy. And smothery.

Not very good at describing.

'Tillie,' said Dr Ev, squeezing back into her chair, 'tell me. Are you sleeping?'

'Not so well.'

'Uh-huh. Waking up, how often?'

Don't know, she thought. Don't even know if I've slept.

'A few times.'

Dr Ev tapped the keyboard on her laptop. 'Okay,' she said, 'how's the diet?'

'No different. Um, pasta, chicken –'

'Varied?'

'I guess. We have vegetables.' Her mother's insistence; sermons on the sacredness of greens.

'Exercise?'

'Some.' As in walk to school, walk home. Most days.

'Cycle?'

'No, walking –'

'Sweetie, I meant your menstrual cycle.'

'Oh. Um, normal.'

'Good. What about the other side? Are you regular?'

Tillie's face must have betrayed her, because Dr Ev smiled, patted Tillie's arm and said, 'I don't want a description. I just want to know if your body is functioning as it should.'

'Yes,' she said, 'I'm regular.'

'Good. Now, total honesty please. Are you taking anything?'

'As in –'

'Drugs. Tillie, I have to ask. Full picture –'

'No. Headache tablets occasionally, but not –'

'Alcohol?'

Once, she thought guiltily, start of last year's summer break, Macy's father lunching at a restaurant, his cabinet filled with those vivid colours and adult labels and Macy urging, just a sip, one little sip, won't hurt, maybe another … At home later that afternoon her mother had smelled Tillie's breath, seen her glassy eyes and exploded, volcanic rage.

Henry: 'Susan, calm down! It's okay. She's made a mistake –'

Susan: 'It is not okay! It's not!'

Banging doors and sobbing; her mother's wrenching sobs were scarier than her anger.

Susan again: 'You *know* why it's not okay!'

'Tillie?' Dr Ev, touching her elbow.

'Sorry.'

'Alcohol. I don't care if you've tried it. I'm asking, do you drink, and if so, how often?'

'I don't. I mean, I have –'

'Experimentation but nothing more?'

'Yes,' she said, relieved.

Tap-tap. The printer whirred and Dr Ev fixed Tillie with eyes that were as dark and gritty as a dust storm.

'Tillie,' she said in a gentle but all-knowing manner, 'clearly you are a well-adjusted, normal young lady. Physically, you're as fit as any fifteen-year-old should be. However, the human body has a delicate chemistry. Sometimes our various oils and gels can become unbalanced. If that happens, emotions can be affected.' She smiled encouragingly and said, 'Usually happy people can become unusually sad.'

Tillie nodded.

Dr Ev said, 'Now, this state of imbalance may simply pass as your body adjusts, or you may need some further diagnosis if it persists. But what I'd really like to happen here is for Tillie Bassett to get some sleep.'

'I'd like that too,' said Tillie.

'You're healthy,' said Dr Ev, 'and as yet there's no obvious, identifiable reason for your sadness, so I think we should focus on the sleep and take a wait-and-see approach with the rest. Agreed?'

She handed over a prescription before Tillie could answer.

'Sedative,' she said. 'Mild but effective. One a night, half an hour before bed. No more than one, okay?'

'Okay.'

'See you in a fortnight, lovely. How are Mum and Dad?'

'Fine,' said Tillie. She assumed so, didn't really know.

'Come on!' urged Macy. 'The park!'

Tall, cool, American, emerald eyes, deep swoon of a voice, athletic, generous – all that she was not, thought Tillie, and yet somehow Macy had chosen her as Best Friend, Tillie still not believing it, thinking now that maybe Macy was Tigger and she was Eeyore.

Macy hustled down the pavements, so Tillie did her best to hustle with her, the girls toiling to avoid hipsters projecting their frappés and active-wear acolytes power-walking prams filled with Harpers and Arabellas. Macy's second-favourite spot in the whole wide world was New Farm Park – her first was Central Park in New York, heaven, thought Tillie, to ever go there – but New Farm Park, two buses away from Red Hill, was semi-heaven with its vast lawn and English-style bandstand, rose gardens flanked by trellised walk-throughs and trees, giant figs and the famous Brisbane jacarandas that blossomed into a mesmerising cloud of mauve every spring.

Now, however, was late March and typically autumn, bright and breezy. The wind was fluking in different directions and the jacarandas were shedding their tiny mustard leaves. Macy insisted on eating bags of chips, dangling their feet over the brown river.

'So,' she said.

'So,' Tillie agreed.

'This is nice,' said Macy. 'This is a good Sunday.'

Tillie looked at Macy as Macy looked at a ferry arriving at the nearby terminal. Her friend was from Philadelphia. She had come to Brisbane with her father, a financier with one of the Big Banks, and been immediately regarded with great suspicion by the Year Nine cohort at Canondale College. Typical American, they'd whispered not so discreetly. Loudmouth. Wants to be the centre of attention. Total pain in the doodad. But Macy was not like that. She'd fitted like an egg into a cup, joined without taking over and hardly ever – never, really – talked about exotic, other-worldly America or her life there. Most importantly, thought Tillie, Macy stayed true, like a jacaranda that remained forever in springtime. She was warm and flowery and playful and she was *that* colour.

She knew about the sadness. Tillie had told her, a hushed phone call two nights ago.

'Guessed there was something,' Macy had said. 'God, we humans are *so* complex. Gorgeous with it, of course. Want me to come over?'

Sunday, they'd agreed. Now Macy said firmly, 'Tillie, we will get you through this.'

We. Not 'You'll get through this' – you, alone, do whatever you can, maybe recover, maybe not. *We*.

Don't ever leave me, Macy. Be my Best Friend, by my side, for always.

Macy flicked a chip towards a patrol squad of seagulls. They squabbled and pecked until one emerged and fled across the river with its feast.

'The thing is,' said Macy, 'it's realistic. To be sad. You know, there's so much dumb stuff in the world – wars, disasters, terrorists, those poor refugees, it actually makes sense to be sad.'

Makes sense ... Macy, trying to make her feel better, normal –

'My guess is that you've got this massive social conscience thing happening. You're sad because the world is pretty much a sad place.'

Yes, it was – but surely that was the world, not her? Oh, there was fear, of course there was, but fear didn't necessarily progress to hopelessness, did it? She wondered, though, did everyone else have those same terrible visions of screaming terrorists with their black masks and cold eyes in slits? Did other people see them slithering into Australia, their guns pumping death into malls and shopping centres and public parks –

'No,' said Tillie quietly. 'No, I do care about those things but I can't – it'd be wrong to claim them as a reason.'

'Really? Did you see the picture of that little boy!'

Tillie shook her head, no, what little boy – and Macy explained, a child washed up on a beach, drowned as he and two hundred others, fleeing the thieves and murderers who stalked their bombed-out homes, tried to cross the Mediterranean Sea and find safety somewhere. Anywhere.

Sick-making. The girls put down their chips: it seemed wrong to eat.

Eventually Tillie said, 'The doctor thinks it's chemical.'

'Oh, everything's chemical,' said Macy, pushing back her mane of honey hair. 'The world's a chemical madhouse. Chemicals in the earth, chemicals in the oceans and water and air, chemicals in animals, chemicals in us, chemicals in the chemicals! Of course it's chemical.'

'So –'

'So, that's kind of obvious but it's not an answer. Look, the way I see it, the big stuff, politics, wars, poverty – those things are definitely sad. But there's still plenty of small stuff to be happy about.'

'Such as?'

'Here,' said Macy, waving her arms. 'There. Just – stuff.'

Tillie said, 'You always seem so happy.'

Check-back needed. Had she sounded accusatory? Envious?

'Not always,' said Macy.

'Yes,' Tillie insisted. She couldn't think of a time –

'Not always.' This time Macy spoke to the wind and it sounded harsh, Tillie surprised until her friend laughed and said more brightly, 'But hey, I give it a go. I definitely give it a go! Like, look at that kid over there, chasing her dog. Look at the dumbo birds. Look at …'

Maybe she kept listing, Tillie didn't know. Dying leaves brushed her hair as she drifted and thought, Macy's right. Small stuff. Concentrate on that, be happy for that.

Didn't work.

Because when you decide to look at nothing but the small

stuff, naturally you start to look more closely, look a bit smaller then look within, bite down on the detail, and that's when you see blemishes that are not so beautiful, not like you'd thought they might be – kind of ugly in fact, and ugliness is an easy convert to sadness, when there are blemishes everywhere –

Starting with herself.

Tillie had never really liked mirrors – as a small child she had been frightened of them – but the walls of their house were home to many in a bewildering variety of frames: plain, rococo, gilt, trapezoidal, oval, Roman, floral, carved, mosaic. Susan's obsession with mirrors had been built to match her obsession for constantly checking and admonishing her choose-your-own-adventure hair.

The gleaming, full-length bathroom mirror was the worst. It menaced Tillie.

Because it wasn't just her knees that were shapeless. She was shapeless all over. Tillie the paper bag. The half-puffed balloon.

And dowdy. Why did she look so – so nothing? Colourless eyes, mousey hair that might as well be chopped off and stuffed into a chair, like they used to do in the olden days before the invention of proper stuffing. That lifeless, pasty skin like a slap-down of dough that needed to be baked or at least flavoured – roll in some raisins or choc drops, anything to make it textured. Even her lips ... colourless, she thought, as if the blood never bothered to flow there. Paper lips, folded and silent.

That was it. She wasn't a person, she was origami made from the last page in the last pad.

Tillie took to draping a spare towel over the bathroom

mirror, but elsewhere the small stuff continued to let her down. One evening she sat in the family room to watch TV with her parents. Re-runs of last decade's fave music quiz show. They always watched it so Susan and Henry could out-point each other on the questions, Susan insisting on double points for her correct answers because Henry naturally knew more, being practically old enough to have gone to school with Beethoven. They both liked to use Tillie as a reference point whenever the questions went dude-ish, like hip hop or electronica – not that she knew, but her parents seemed to think that her guesses were more likely to be accurate than their own.

Dylan! Bacharach! Nirvana! 1980! Tillie couldn't concentrate. She let her gaze wander from the TV, and that was when she saw it, a lone grey hair sneaking murderously across her mother's temple like a wolf on a plain.

Grey hair.

Age.

Ageing. Moving towards –

Inevitably towards –

Oh, God, thought Tillie desperately ... I want to rush over and hold her but I can't because she'll say, why, why are you squeezing me like this, Tillie. It's very unusual. And I can't tell her, I can't say, Mum, because you've got a grey hair, that's just dumb. Can't say that I just realised you're probably closer to dying than being born. My mother dying, it's unbearable and grainy and black –

She blinked away the tears. Looked desperately at her father for solace – and saw that there were creases in his profile that she'd never noticed before, flesh bunching and bulging, a heaviness across his middle. He's older too, she thought, but that must be wrong – Henry has always been early forties. She'd been answering that way for years … How old's your dad? Oh, early forties. Five years ago, seven, ten – no, she thought, no, terrible daughter, I don't even know how old he is –

The small stuff, conspiring. And yes, it was irrational, of course it was, but she couldn't help, couldn't stop –

Tillie went to bed early, swallowed her sleeping pill, lay stiff and tense and open-eyed.

Off school for a day, two. The sleeping pills, she told them. Flattened her, ongoing drowsiness.

Susan said briskly, 'I'll call Dr Ev.'

'No.' Tillie yawned before adding, 'I'll be fine. She said there might be some side effects.'

'Doing it now,' Susan told her.

Important? Yes, but not classifiable as urgent, appointment next week. Her mother scuttled irritably into her studio, her father into his study, and Tillie wandered the house, touching objects and wondering about their origins. What would happen to these things when they, the family, were all gone … Where did things go? People might inherit and try to preserve them but sooner or later objects fall apart or crumble, to be thrown on to a scrap heap or buried. Eventually it all breaks down to dust and that dust becomes the new earth or is blown into the sky or ocean, but it doesn't just disappear – it still exists, each tiny granule, so how can there be room for all the dust that used to be castles and villages and aqueducts and trees and prehistoric animals and medieval people –

Neither awake nor asleep … Mid-afternoon she answered the doorbell and found Snake, pale-faced and awkward, in the portico. She was in her pyjamas, hadn't bothered to shower or change.

Later. Whatever. She hid her frumpy, papery self behind the door.

'Um, hi.'

Snake was holding his schoolbag in front, as if it were a gift. He said, 'Hey,' blinked big a couple of times then said, 'haven't seen you for a while.'

'Sick,' Tillie told him.

'Oh. Not good.'

She twitched. 'Just tired,' she said.

He nodded, and Tillie thought, I should ask him in, usually do. We've know each other for a long time. Since we were littlies, shared a fence until his parents had child number five – the one before Jackson – and needed a bigger house. So we've shared heaps. And pyjamas are no big deal. Back then we were kids in PJs, riding our pretend-unicorns and beating back pretend-monsters –

Why not ask him in?

Can't. Nothing to do with pyjamas, everything to do with effort. She could hear their potential dialogue jackhammering inside her skull. You okay? Yeah, sort of … No, not really. What is it? Sad. Why? Don't know? Can I help? No. I'm your friend, I want to help. No, don't worry about it. Please? Snake, no. Tillie, we've been friends since ... Please, Snake, I said no. No!

Erosion. Don't want that.

'Sorry,' she said. 'Supposed to be resting.'

'Sure.' Snake goofed her a smile, always crinkly, always meant. He looked ready to go, until he said, 'I just wanted to make sure you were okay.'

'Will be.' Tillie tried to return the smile but it was half-baked, best she could do. Those papery lips would be dust one day, trodden into the earth or blown into the emptiness ...

'And tell you something,' he continued. 'An idea I had.'

Save the world, no doubt. Snake's ideas were always about that. Let's do a fun run for world poverty. Stitch malaria tents and send them to Africa. Visit some libraries and get free books and ship them to Timor-Leste because, did you know, the literacy rate there is less than forty per cent and that's terrible – there's no hope for improvement unless –

'It's okay,' Snake told her. 'We can talk later. When you're feeling better.'

She felt guilty. 'Actually,' she said, 'now would be –' but he was waving away her concerns, saying, 'Honestly, it's no big deal. Save it.'

Tillie bowed her head. Snake seemed to be on the verge of raising one leg, like a flamingo. They stayed for a moment in that two-person space where nothing happens because neither can initiate, then Snake said, 'Actually, it's a computer game. I could, um, inbox you the details?'

'Please. And sorry, I'm just –'

'Hey, no problem.'

He wandered away, reaching the footpath before turning, making a phone with his hand and calling out, 'If you need anything –'

'Thanks!' Tillie watched him go, her oldest friend, the one they'd all called Snake because he'd been short and tubby and the name was a joke, meant to be ironic, not especially clever. He'd never minded, or had never seemed to – which one, she wasn't sure.

On Sunday morning Susan suggested a laughter club, and Tillie immediately thought no, ridiculous notion, laughing because other people were, for no actual reason. Just laughing, as if the act was somehow disconnected from a source, like a joke. Was there a shouting club, a burping club? And how could anyone possibly manufacture, from nothing –

Causal?

On the way down Windsor Road they passed Mrs Cooper, their near-neighbour. She lived alone in a cottage, had bad legs and partial blindness. Susan took her casseroles for the freezer and did her washing and cleaning every week.

Once Tillie had asked her mother … why choose to help an old woman who was neither relative nor close friend? There must be other people who could –

'There's not,' Susan had said shortly.

But why her, Tillie had persisted. Why Mrs Cooper ahead of anyone else? Susan had chosen to not reply, Tillie backing down, sensing that her mother was irritated.

Embarrassed?

About choosing Mrs Cooper?

Or about showing compassion?

The park, part of the university, was hunched between apartment blocks, making the air still and humid. Tillie saw a dozen or so people gathered in a circle, mostly women in bulgy black leggings and baggy tees. One woman broke from the circle and welcomed Susan and Tillie. There was a skittish wind in the welcomer's voice, as if she hadn't ever settled on a rhythm or tone.

There was a moment until, without warning, the woman spun back to the group and laughed. It could have been a magpie swooping and hollering, but no one seemed to mind because they were laughing too. A bearded man across the circle from Tillie was already bent at the waist, bellowing and snorting and holding himself, as if the laughter might explode from his belly in an arc, like a rainbow fizz.

The whole set-up was bizarre.

Tillie moved her feet, made patterns in the dew ... recognised that deepish up-and-down scale favoured by her mother. Susan was also laughing. They were all laughing – except Tillie.

So it went for the next fifteen minutes or so, a collection of noise that made Tillie, standing alone, think of the sea, such was its roll and tempest. Wave after wave, deep currents, tidal shifts, rogue ripples, plinking and swooshing, slapping, crashing –

'Tillie,' said her mother, 'it's over. Come on.'

Susan's face was creased and red; she looked like she had just woken. They walked briskly to the car, but Susan did not immediately turn the ignition and zoom away without checking or indicating, as was her habit.

'You're not,' she said, the sentence stalling before – 'You're not trying.'

Tillie said nothing. Unfair, she thought. I didn't laugh because there was nothing to laugh about, and it's crazy to behave like that for the sake of it, especially with a bunch of weirdo strangers –

Susan said, 'Was it really that bad? I saw the ad, thought it might be fun, a good thing to do together. Bonding on a Sunday morning. Then you just stand there –'

'Sorry.'

'Sourpuss look on your face –'

'I said I'm sorry!'

Breathe, breathe. Tillie felt her mother's exasperation … then her fingers creeping and tightening across Tillie's hand.

Pause.

Susan said in a calmer tone, 'Sometimes you just have to get on with it. You know? Don't overthink. Just do.'

'Mum,' said Tillie, 'I know you meant well, but that, I can't –'

'Can't laugh? Can't enjoy yourself for the sake of it? Of course you can. Everyone can, if they want to. But I'm not sure that you –'

Want to? You think I'm *pretending* to be sad?

'Home,' said Susan, with a sigh. Her skin was blotchy, eyes crinkling, the laughter utterly evaporated. 'Bad mother needs a coffee,' she added.

When a gecko darted from the air con unit on her bedroom wall to the window, Tillie thought that she might write a poem. The tense sky had finally flexed its afternoon muscles, the day turning to magenta and pewter. There was a rumour of hail lurking beneath the heavens, so Tillie's father moved his beloved Moke undercover while her mother hurried to the back porch with her camera, set up a tripod and snapped madly.

All of this while the gecko paused on the narrow pelmet. Tillie wondered if the animal had been forced inside by the unsettled air. Maybe it was seeking food? Maybe simply exploring? Either way, she liked the gecko and wanted to write about it so she sat in her chair, opened the screen of her laptop and looked to the window for inspiration.

But the gecko had gone.

Suddenly anxious, she scanned the walls. Not there. She stood on her bed and checked the slit entrances and dusty case of the air conditioner.

Not there.

The floor? Beneath the bed? The furniture?

None of these, and now she could feel the creature's absence beginning to overpower her. The emptiness of the walls was as rough and painful as an abrasion … Oh, she was sad. Terribly, foolishly, why-why-why sad, she thought, striking at her left leg. Stupidly sad, pathetically sad – striking at her right leg and pinching her elbow. It was just a gecko – pinch harder! Make it hurt! They were common as muck – pinch again, dig your nails, make it bleed! – a dumb gecko, a pest – pinch! PINCH! So why –

Why are you weeping? Why do you hurt yourself? Why do your lungs shrink and reject the air? Why do you want to take those scissors from the top drawer and –

Just a gecko just a gecko. Gecko gecko gecko. Gecko echo. Sshh.

Tillie left her chair, lay on her bed. Lay very straight. Tightened her nerve ends, kept her hands away from her body and forced herself towards blankness. Do nothing. Think nothing.

Noth-ing.

Finally the tears evaporated. She stopped shaking. Her breathing steadied and her sight returned. She stared up at familiar shapes appearing through the mist ... disappointing. That ceiling fan had dirty edges. There was a stain on the plaster from a leak in the roof two years ago. Three? Four? A long time ago. It should have been fixed. Why wasn't it fixed? When it comes to that, she thought indignantly, why did there have to be dirt and stains? Why couldn't everything stay perfectly, wonderfully white? What sort of messed-up world couldn't maintain a simple, basic whiteness? What was so difficult about –

Noth-ing.

Be still.

Just a gecko.

Breathe ...

Sshh, sshh ... and see the cold-eyed men rising like liquid disruption from the roads, lifting their guns to aim and shoot – at Susan, no, and Henry, no, Rosie, Niko, all of them running and screaming, mercy, mercy, there was Snake, no, and Macy, she'd outrun them, she'd outlast everyone, and behind her, lagging, someone else … it was her, Tillie, that was definitely her, cow eyes, paper lips, big slow body lumbering, falling to the beat of gunfire, beating, beating, unstoppable –

She cried out as she opened her eyes. The room swam. Her phone was jangling, Taylor Swift. Tay-Tay. She didn't even like Taylor Swift, just used the ringtone because people heard, they judged, they commented, you had to coolify the ringtone –

Tillie sat up. Her entire body was hurting, as if she'd overexercised. Ha! Fat chance of that … she picked up the phone, noted the caller ID through the fog and swiped.

'Rosie?'

'Hey, little sis. How's things?'

She knows, thought Tillie. Someone's told her.

Must have been Dad.

'Tillie?'

'Um, okay.'

'Yeah? You sound weird. Are you really okay?'

'I guess.'

'Truth, please.'

Tillie said in a clearer voice, 'Oh, you know. Up and down.' She thought quickly, adding, 'I went to a laughter club this morning.'

Rosie's breath came in a loud exhale. 'Mum?' she asked.

'Mmm.'

'Loves a good fad, our Susan. Hey, we were thinking, you want to come up to the farm next weekend? Niko is promising moussaka.'

Tillie's heart lifted at the prospect: time spent with her sister and Niko, the bonus of his rich moussaka, a salad filled with yummy home-grown tomatoes – and that lovely night-in-the-country peace, frogs croaking their pleasure as they blobbed in the pond and more stars than anyone could count in a lifetime.

'I can ask,' she said hopefully.

'No need,' Rosie told her, 'because I will sort it, pronto. I'll ring Henry. We're down for an appointment anyway so we can pick you up, no problems.'

'Thank you!'

'Easy-peasy. Hey, it'll be fun. We'll play one-hit wonders and do zany girl talk. Oh, and Niko said he wants to teach you how to make dolmades and how to waltz.'

'Really?'

'Sure. Sis, we can do anything. You know what I'm saying?'

Tillie did. Her eye had caught a sudden movement, the gecko spreadeagled like a candle splat on the window pane. As she watched, the animal lifted its head and peered at the world through bug eyes.

'Thanks, Rosie,' said Tillie. Put down her phone, breathed.

The storm passed out to sea, night dropped like a velvet coverlet and insects erupted from the garden, swarms of them batting madly against the screens. Susan, who'd been trying to teach herself to photoshop, came into the lounge room and asked, 'What happened to your arm?'

'Huh?'

'Your arm, Tillie. It's bruised.'

What? Oh, that.

'Caught it in a cupboard,' she said. 'Pinched it.'

'Ice?'

'It's okay.' Tillie gave the flesh a quick rub. 'Doesn't hurt.'

Liar, liar. Susan didn't look too convinced but she'd left the room when Tillie's father breezed in, dangled his car keys and said to her, 'Let's go.'

He was as rumpled and multi-coloured as a bed quilt. Old habits – back when he was employed by State Arts, Henry had decided to wear op-shop clothes throughout the weekend as a form of passive protest; at work, a new boss had insisted that he wear a tie when he had not done so in ten years.

A tie, Henry had grumbled. Colonial jackboot, relic of Western imperialism –

'Keep it loose,' Susan had said wisely.

'I *am* loose. It's him, not me –'

'As in, undo the top button,' Susan told him.

Which he did, in concert with another, more direct protest: making sure that his tie never matched his work shirts or jackets.

Now her father looked eager. Tillie asked, 'Go where?'

'Centro. Did you forget? The Italian film festival.'

They sat in the farthest corner of the third-front row because Henry preferred it – 'My poor old eyes,' he always said, but Tillie knew the real reason: he disliked being close to other patrons, most of whom occupied the middle. It was a conundrum, to love the cinema but dislike those who went there. If she ever won Powerball – and a good start would be to buy a ticket – she'd build Henry his own cinema. There'd be European films screened in utter darkness, no popcorn or choc tops – 'Why do people feel the need to eat just because they're watching a movie?' – definitely no mobile phones and a heavyweight, polar-cap silence. Her father hated whisperers in particular.

'They're not entitled to do that,' he'd retorted to Susan.

'Oh, give over, Henry,' she'd said. 'In this day and age, everyone's entitled to do whatever they want. According to themselves, anyway.'

Susan, at the cinema with friends, was a whisperer.

The film was strange and beautiful. Tillie wanted to love it for her father's sake but she couldn't. An old man in bright jackets wandered around Rome being inspired by the art and architecture. There were surreal images of bridges, statues, novice nuns and enormous birds. There were also lots of parties for people whose dancing was manic. Tillie wondered if the story had been about old age, perhaps love, some intersection of the two, but it was difficult to know.

As she left the cinema, the thought came to her that the Italian film had been an orchid, made for loveliness and little else.

'Coffee?' suggested her father.

A rare treat. They sat at Puccini's, away from the in-crowd. Henry ordered cappuccinos and a wedge of pumpkin pie that he carefully bisected. The pie was delicious, the coffee welcome and at first neither Tillie nor Henry spoke much. She had always loved that about her father – his willingness to embrace comfortable, guilt-free silences.

Somewhere in the distance, a volley of fireworks.

'Well,' said her father, 'the movie. I loved it. You know why? Because the main guy wasn't locked in to anything. He was very random, very cool.'

'He was cool –'

'More than that,' said Henry. 'He was free.'

'Like you,' suggested Tillie.

'Quite the opposite of me,' her father said, lightly earnest. 'Anyway, I loved him and I loved the film. How about you?'

Tillie considered. 'It was pretty,' she said, and Henry grinned.

'Pretty,' he echoed. 'Yes, it was. Though that does sound like a veiled criticism.'

She nodded, gave him her orchid analogy.

Her father stirred the dregs in his cup. He asked, 'What about the music?'

Tillie shrugged. She hadn't really noticed the music, not with that fruity feast of colour to sting her senses.

Her father said in his quiet, serious way, 'Tillie, the music made me ache.'

'Oh,' she said, 'I'm sorry.'

He raised his eyebrows.

'Sorry that you feel that way,' she explained. 'A film has made you ache.'

'But I liked that,' her father told her. 'I *want* a film that makes me ache. That's how I know that it matters, that I care. And if I care –'

She looked at him more closely and had a sense of the old family dog, long nose and ears made to tug, brown skin that

35

was lightly furred, lightly roasted, down-in-the-corner eyes. Curl on the couch, bark when needed.

'If I care,' said Henry, 'then I'm alive.'

Later, in bed, Tillie thought about that, her father making *his* pain sound welcome. The music hurt him but it was a good hurt … She supposed it was possible. Like going to the dentist and being numb in the jaw. She had always detested that particular experience and welcomed the wearing-off as a sign that she was nearly recovered. The onset of discomfort was a relief and much better than feeling nothing, which was definitely scary … She supposed that was the idea behind her father's words. We have to feel, even if that means pain.

Sometime after midnight the rain returned and Tillie dozed on the edge of it, the soft roar, the alternate cleansing and muddying of the world.

She clicked on the link and scanned the synopsis. Snake's game, 'Philanthropy', worked thus: as the sole player you became the character known as Benefactor, a metallic figure that looked like a recoloured Disney animation of a Greek god. Benefactor's goal was to gather credits by climbing mountains, traversing valleys and negotiating a series of labyrinths (this would be the best part of the game, Tillie thought). Once this stage was completed, Benefactor had to get past the Haves – fat scarlet bugs wearing tunics with shimmering dollar signs – using 'cunning and speed.' There were no weapons. If Benefactor did manage to pass the Haves, which had been coded to continuously multiply, then the player's objective was to distribute whatever credits had been gained to a crowd of Have-nots (oddly endearing cartoon-mouths) by pressing Control/Down arrow and letting those credits, tiny corn cobs, drop into their mouths – whereupon the Have-nots would smile and Benefactor would regather strength, seen through a health bar that hovered overhead like a luminous lime zeppelin. Smiling Have-nots vanished – Benefactor's goal being to empty the Have-not arena – but of course the Haves were still multiplying, meaning that the game had to be restarted …

Hope you like it, Snake had written. *Just an idea. Early stages. Lots to do.*

Wanting so much to please him, Tillie typed back: *It's amazing. Come around sometime and we'll test it together.*

Sometime. Should she have been more specific?

Too late, message sent. And delivered. And read. Oh, how quick the world …

At her mother's urging she tried school again but was home before lunch.

'This,' said Susan, 'this is ─'

Tillie said dolefully, 'I know, I'm sorry.'

She ground her toes into the carpet. She wanted to explain, but looking back made it seem so ridiculous, beginning with that moment when she left her father in the car at the front gates of the college and idly, stupidly, wondered, is that it? Will I ever see him again? See Susan? Or will something happen while I'm here … my parents will leave for a well-earned, extended break from their nutty daughter or they'll simply disappear. People did that, gone without a trace, bedroom left the same as usual, letters spilling like weeds into the garden.

The car had returned to traffic and she'd stood alone on the asphalt while more rubbish crowded into that hot, crammed space known as her brain … The police would come because there'd been a car accident, a fire in the studio, a murderer in the study. Terrorists, stalking the streets! Oh, God … Tillie had forced herself into the grounds and tried to channel different thoughts, but that hadn't worked either; seeing Ms Graham, who'd waved, seeing a tribe of tiny Year Sevens loping along beneath enormous backpacks like ants carrying loaves, seeing Georgia Eccles waiting patiently outside the computer fix-it lab, groups rushing eagerly to the handball courts, a Year Twelve boy knocking on the library door – she'd stopped and thought, don't any of you realise? Don't you know? This is it! One life, who knows how many days or hours, minutes, seconds, then you'll be dust and it will all be for nothing –

Susan asked sharply, 'Tillie? Did something happen?'

Ridiculous! She'd gone to her locker, Colette Jarvis had said in a pleasant voice, 'Hey, stranger,' and Tillie had begun to cry. So stupid, embarrassing … but Macy had buzzed in like a jet fighter and told Colette to shove off, leave Tillie alone. There'd been sharp words, Colette protesting her innocence in rising falsetto, Macy labelling her as insensitive and, moments later, face-jammed-against-face, a moron. Homeroom passed in a blur – Tillie not hearing her name at roll-call but someone must have answered for her – then she couldn't remember her timetable and had forgotten her diary so she'd gone to the wrong classroom, a bunch of Year Elevens comparing the victories and losses of their weekends. A teacher, she didn't know who, probably a replacement, had suggested she go to the office, but Ms Andrewartha had swung by and said, 'It's okay, Tillie, I'm late too,' and they'd gone into drama together, Tillie's lungs compressing into small, hard nuggets as she scanned the room. Look at you all, she'd thought, don't you realise? Dust, black dust, ground into the earth, blown by the wind … Everyone else was already in groups, already doing their scenes from *Romeo and Juliet,* and Ms Andrewartha said, 'Sorry, Tillie, we weren't sure when you were returning. How about a monologue? Juliet's wedding song, *Gallop apace* … would be perfect –'

She could hear her mother barking into her phone. 'Now, if possible – yes, I'm aware of that but I think – surely there's a spot somewhere? A cancellation, or – yes. Yes, fine. Thank you.'

Gallop apace … she knew the speech, took out the book, but couldn't see it to read, the words running and jumping as if they too were part of a scheme designed to confound her. Ms Andrewartha glanced over but she was busy with pretentious Aidan Fletcher who thought he was the new DiCaprio … Somehow Tillie had found herself sitting in the darkened wings of the stage that adjoined the classroom, an airless tomb where the flats and props were stored. The *Godspell* stuff was in one corner next to kaftans, scarves and *stuff* in labelled boxes. She was crying without noise or rhythm and rubbing her cheeks with a green clown's wig when Ms Andrewartha poked her head past the curtain and said, 'There you are,' Tillie frozen to the moment as if she'd been caught committing a crime. She'd begun to apologise profusely – 'Miss, I'm sorry, so sorry, I wasn't thinking, sorry!' – and that was when she'd been walked back to Transition like some poor sap on Death Row. But Allegra was at a conference and the other lady, Mrs Marsden, professional cardigan-wearer, said it was *best practice* and certainly more *appropriate* to keep each case separated – now she was a *case* – so Mrs Marsden rang the office, which rang Susan, who picked up Tillie and brought her home.

'Come on,' said her mother briskly. 'They've moved things around. You have an appointment with Dr Ev.'

They sat together in the waiting room, Susan alternating between scoffing at suggestions in a homemaker magazine – 'Checked curtains, who would do that?' – and glancing at her phone. Tillie looked around the room. Something to fix on, she thought, an anchor to stop my drift –

A man came in, late twenties, maybe thirty. He gave his name to the receptionist and sat near Kiddies' Corner. The man's crew cut was washing-powder white, stark against tanned skin and a shirt wildly patterned with red and blue violins. Tillie watched as he folded himself neatly into his seat, reached into a canvas satchel and produced a Rubik's Cube.

He began by swivelling the edges of the cube, his fingers working so quickly that Tillie could not follow. As well as manipulating the various sections, the man frequently turned the entire cube, caressing, inspecting, rolling; she was reminded of Niko kneading dough for bread. Soon she gave up watching the blur of the man's fingers and followed the colours instead. A panel became fully green before he disrupted it by clicking in squares of white and blue, these becoming rectangles, a block of five ... the red was mostly done then undone, orange seemed to be a problem –

'Tillie?'

Dr Ev, blocking the light.

She heard her mother's sigh of relief as they stood, Tillie heard herself say to the man, 'That's amazing.'

He looked up, smiled and mouthed a silent *thanks* – which was when she saw a thick bandage patched across the right side of his throat.

'Depression,' said Susan Bassett firmly, a few minutes later. 'She needs a referral.'

'Not yet.' Dr Ev had re-examined Tillie, declared her well enough, if perhaps a little underweight, and redefined her crying as *episodes*.

'The episode this morning, a trigger perhaps ... the last episode, similar trigger –'

No, thought Tillie. No episodes. State of being. Gecko gecko ... She felt cold and alone, lying on a couch in her undies and bra while her mother and her doctor batted theories back and forth in a game of medical table tennis. Anyway, she'd worked it out, sort of ... I'm a sad person, she thought. By destiny, by draw. There are happy people and angry people, curious people, unfortunate people, mad, ambitious, unfeeling, driven. I'm sad. I've probably always been sad but you don't notice how you are when you're a little kid because everything is new and therefore unknown, including emotions –

Wouldn't it be useful, she thought, if we could be identified by colour … sad people could have blue skin, yellow for happy, red for angry – which sometimes happened anyway, like Mr O'Brien the maths teacher, turning beetroot whenever the Year Eights started their carry-on. Maybe green for curious? Or was that envious? Dear Google, what colour is curious? And what about unfortunate? When blue's already taken –

'Mindfulness,' said Dr Ev.

'Oh, I don't know.' Exasperated, Susan shook her hair. She said, 'Tillie, what do you think?'

That it's too cold in here, the couch smells of disinfectant and why isn't the wall perfectly white? Gecko gecko … I wish I hadn't worn these undies because the elastic's nearly gone and Dr Ev really should have purple skin, the colour of omnipotence –

'Okay,' she mumbled.

On the way out she noticed that the man with the Rubik's Cube was gone. Tillie hoped that he would be okay, that the patch on his throat wasn't covering a hole through which his voice had escaped for all time. She'd liked the way he'd manipulated the cube. Liked his competence, his obvious pleasure in his craft.

Liked his happiness.

Rosie and Niko's farm was piecemeal, always developing, never finished. This riled Susan, whose only visit had ended with a comment – unfortunately overheard – about Rosie's 'drop-out' lifestyle choices. Not surprisingly an argument had followed, but then Rosie and her mother had never been at ease. Tillie could remember a distant time when Rosie had stormed bullishly out of Henry's study yelling, 'I can't, I won't!' When wide-eyed, unknowing Tillie had asked, 'Can't-won't-what?' Rosie had thundered, 'I hate her!' before rushing on to the street and running away for fifteen taut, difficult hours.

Niko parked the jeep beneath an awning and the three of them wandered the surrounds, Tillie, as always, looking forward to the fresh smells and tomato plants stretching over their wires, the imperfect rows of fruit trees, Zeus spinning on his doggy bum in anticipation of being fed, the free-ranging chooks – Grizabella, champion layer! – and rusting sheds, the empty barn sitting quietly on the farm's distant, western edge, the canvas of paddocks like stitched-together pieces of light, the purple brow of the horizon and storm-shattered gums. She needed to see the whole panorama in order to reassure herself that this magical place was still here, still real.

In the car she'd told them of her most recent visit to Dr Ev ... sleeping tablets taken away, a new regimen of natural supplements.

'What, herbal?'

'I think so. Magnesium. Thea ... thea-something.'

'Theanine?' asked Niko, turning down the radio.

'Um, maybe. Think so.'

'Glory be,' said Rosie, rolling her eyes dramatically. 'How did our mother cope with that?'

'Not so well,' admitted Tillie. 'She was pushing for something more –'

'Artificial, potent and addictive?'

'I'm not sure,' said Tillie diplomatically. She added, 'Mum's worried, I guess.'

Rosie sniffed at that, so Tillie explained about the mindfulness program that she would be undertaking as of next week: body-scanning, learning to breathe in a more focused way, meditation.

'Dr Ev recommended that?'

'Yes. And yoga.'

Rosie was obviously surprised, as Tillie had been. Dr Ev had built a practice around her no-nonsense approach. Got an ailment? Bang, here's a solution. Mind therapy was a long way from prescriptions for antibiotics and stern lectures about diet.

They left the cooling air and went into the kitchen – pine shelves, long-stemmed plants in vases, faded recipes pinned into the walls – where, as promised, Niko showed Tillie how to fold dolmades, the leaves rolled delicately around fragrant pellets of mince. Rosie's fiancé was a big man, bearish, with a wobbling smile and very dark hair spread on his forearms like Vegemite. Older than Rosie by nine years, he'd been a TV cameraman filming a group protesting about coal seam gas mining when he'd first spotted her, microphone in hand, condemning the greedy government. Three months later Niko had tossed his career, bought the farm and pledged himself to organic self-sufficiency.

Her sister, thought Tillie, could be very persuasive.

While Niko assembled the moussaka they went into the adjoining room. Rosie switched on the TV and channel-surfed while Tillie checked her sister's profile, the small perfections of her nose and chin given contrast by the thin, wavering scar that Rosie never spoke about. It began near enough to the corner of her right eye to distort the lid before contouring upwards, eventually becoming lost in her hairline like a disused track in a forest.

Another memory. 'Mum, what happened to Rosie's face?'

'An accident. A long time ago. Now –'

'What accident?'

'She fell into a glass door. Eat up.'

'How did she fall?'

'Tripped. Tillie, peas and carrots, now.'

Tillie closed her eyes. Home was elsewhere and the moussaka smelled delicious.

Rosie asked, 'Any preferences?'

'No.'

'Mind if we catch up with the news?'

Bland at first, the lead being about a politician who had resigned after gifting his nephew a high-paying government job, but it was the next story that clawed at Tillie, a farmer having shot his wife and children before committing suicide. An image of the family smiling as they sat near last year's Christmas tree was especially disturbing because it was so usual: the little boy playing with a toy tractor could have been from any family, so too the girl with her reindeer smock and shiny, sticky-out plaits. The pretty mother had her hand on her husband's shoulder and he, the killer, had his own hand laid gently on the little boy's arm.

She thought, how could this be? What happens in people's lives that they switch from love to savagery? Dust. Oh, God, dust … Rosie pointed the remote and blacked the screen.

'Why take the kids?' she said angrily. 'What've those poor kids done?'

Tillie couldn't reply. Rosie crawled across the couch and hugged her, Tillie pulling back the tears by concentrating on the smell of Rosie's skin, an odd blend of perfume and potatoes.

'Hey, MooMoo, glad you're here. So glad.'

Tillie murmured, 'You haven't called me that in ages.'

'I know,' said Rosie, 'I should remember to do so.' She stretched out, eyed Tillie and said, 'That look you had when you were a bub was so incredibly big and trusting. Dad and I agreed, you were like a newborn calf, and Mum went off.' She mimicked Susan's outraged tone – 'Don't you compare my baby to a common animal!' – before laughing and saying, 'I got sent to my room for a decade while Dad copped the whole shebang, stupid man, useless father, blah-blah.'

Tillie bit her lip.

'She was very protective of you,' mused Rosie. 'I mean, beyond-normal protective.'

'Was she?'

'Oh, yes. Always.'

'Why?'

Rosie considered.

'Two reasons, I think,' she said. 'Of course, you were a few weeks premmie, very small and fragile –'

Not now, thought Tillie, thinking of fat knees and blobby arms, the lump forced into putting towels over mirrors.

'But that wasn't the main reason,' said Rosie. She moved back in to nuzzle her sister's shoulder. 'I think – she wanted to mould you. Our mother needed a daughter who would like her, maybe even love her. That was never going to be me, Tillie, so it had to be you.'

They sat on the verandah, watching the last light trickling bronze across the D'Aguilar Range. True to her promise, Rosie did click into her iTunes collection of one-hit wonders, introducing each new song with a cry of 'Ha!' or 'Niko, remember this one?' Tillie didn't know the songs but she watched and listened as her sister cradled Zeus's dipping head and brayed, 'Who let the dogs out?' then sang about a girl called Tiffany who was offering breakfast to her friends. A short time later, when Niko asked Tillie to dance – very formal, arm outstretched, plummy accent – she arose to his hands and tried to follow the beat as Niko crooned the chorus, which was about someone crying inside a chapel then being happy.

They armchair-danced as Rosie insisted on playing Leonard Cohen – 'Is Dad still mad for old Lennie? He used to play the CDs over and over.' The songs were vaguely familiar from Tillie's early childhood, one about a waltz, another about praying hallelujah. Niko suggested that you could only dance neck-up to Leonard Cohen, which was a funny idea, wobbling your head like a bird gone crazy … Tillie wanted to dance neck-up, wanted to laugh too but she couldn't because of a sense, come upon her with the secrecy and slyness of gas, that it was all beginning to fade. Soon this lovely time on the verandah would be gone; the night would no longer be as royal and glorious as a king's robe, Zeus would stop snuffling into Niko's feet, her sister's wildly exaggerated joy would dwindle … The music would drop to noise then silence and Tillie would be cold again, sad again and wishing in vain that she could sleep deeply without dreams.

Rosie was kneeling by her side. 'Tillie, come on, tell me. Tell me!'

How to reply?

How to be alive?

'I get scared.'

'Me too,' said Rosie quickly. 'All the time, MooMoo. But that's the way of things. We're people, we get –'

'Which makes me sad,' said Tillie, wondering if that scratchy sound really was her voice. 'The other day I looked at Mum and Dad and I thought, one day you're not going to be here. You're going to' – she could hardly say the word – 'die. Like that family on TV tonight, you're going to be nothing.'

'Tillie –'

'I know it's stupid to think like that but I can't help it – I do and it becomes too much. Then I think the same about other people.'

You. Me.

Her sister's arms, her adult brawn, her warmth. Tillie said,

'I feel sad and I don't know what's first, the fear or the sadness, but they're both there and I can't control them. I just can't. And I don't know why.'

They were silent until Niko said, 'Confusing, hey?'

Tillie nodded. Rosie was stroking her arms. Niko continued in a low, even tone, 'It's not the same but – I felt a bit like that after my grandpa passed away. He'd always been so alive, then he was sick, then he wasn't here any more. It happened really quickly, and I just couldn't see how the world could ever be the same. Properly balanced, you know? Or how I could live in a place where he wasn't.'

He sighed and said, 'That made me afraid.'

A sound penetrated; it might have been the cry of a koel.

'So this place' – Niko spread his arms as if to enfold the night – 'is a tribute to my grandpa and the way he lived … I think, for me, that's the purpose, you know, of being here. On the planet. Remembering what they did, what they gave us, and building on it –'

'So, stuff the fears,' said Rosie hotly.

'Yes, but with dignity,' said Niko.

One more song, 'Lullaby'. Tillie had heard it often enough on the radio so they all sang along, the frogs too, and the insects. Even Zeus offered a chorusy murmur before dropping back to his doze.

Tillie's room was a louvred sleepout stretching the southern length of the farmhouse. Sometime after midnight Rosie padded in, sat on the edge of the bed, smoothed Tillie's hair and said, 'Hey, MooMoo, keep a secret?'

'Mmm ...'

Rosie touched her own stomach as if each finger were a silver moth landing on a sill. Tillie waited for her sister to lean down then, she closed her eyes as Rosie whispered sweet words, welcome words.

She felt it as she unlocked the front door, a difference of some sort. Disturbed air, a realignment of the sonar –

Macy's voice, coming from the lounge room.

'Mrs B, it will help, I'm sure it will –'

Tillie left her overnight bag in the hall, opened the connecting door. Her mother, looking hassled and worn behind the protective apron that she used in her studio, was sitting primly on a chair that she had recently repolished and re-covered. Henry was standing with his back to the wood-burning heater while Macy was perched on the couch. Clad in white singlet, bottle-green leggings, and runners, she looked as clean and pure as freshly picked fruit.

Tillie blinked and realised. Macy was holding –

A dog?

'No,' said Susan firmly. Then, lifting her eyes, 'Oh, Tillie, you're back.'

The story emerged in a series of swift grabs and counter-grabs. Macy had taken it upon herself to go to the animal refuge and extricate a puppy, a fox terrier, as a gift for Tillie because dogs were cool, dogs helped you feel good. In fact, if she and Daddy-dearest didn't have to live in a boxy little apartment then Macy would have two, no three, a whole family of her own to help her stay upbeat because dogs do that, they can lift you from the lowest of doldrums to the peakiest of peaks. Yes, said Henry, yes, I agree … No, said Susan, dogs were loud and messy, they pooped all over and they interfered. With what, asked her husband. With us, Susan insisted, we have a certain lifestyle. A well-established lifestyle; we are a no-dog family, that much is obvious. Rare in Brisbane to be a no-dog family, but nevertheless … We could change, said Henry. It's not too late. Never too late … They're cute, said Macy persuasively, and this one is extra cute. I know what you're saying, Mrs B, about lifestyle, 'cause my dad has said the same thing, but you can just train them easy enough and muzzle them if you have to, book them into a kennel if you go away, no probs, you know? There, said Henry, you heard it here, no probs … I'd like a dog. I always wanted one as a kid, but my father – anyway, I'd like one now. More to the point, I'd like Tillie to have one –

'No,' said Susan firmly. 'We're already overloaded. We don't need a dog.'

The fences, she said, the gardens, the time, the expense –

'Macy,' said Tillie, after the retelling had subsided and the puppy had scampered beneath the couch to whimper and scratch, 'you're very kind –'

'But?'

'I'm sorry, I can't.'

Because she knew how much she would love it, and how difficult that love would become, particularly when what-might-happen did happen. Would happen! Like Greta Willard's dog, bitten and killed by an eastern brown when they took it camping … and the little dog from the house down the road that jumped out an open window, ran on to the road and fell into a drain where the grid had been displaced. Never seen again, despite the family plastering posters all over telegraph poles and shop windows. Ever since, the dog's owner, George or John or Jeremy, had walked with his head down, and Tillie knew why: George-John-Jeremy was feeling not just the grief but the responsibility … should've closed the window, should've been watching, should've got Dad to tell the council to fix that grid, should've done this, should've done that –

Should've, a terrible form of self-destruction.

'I thought you'd love it,' said Macy. Her face was suddenly, uncharacteristically lined. She added, 'I thought –' then looked away, said no more.

'I'm sorry,' Tillie said to the floor. 'But I just can't.'

Her father knew. He was kind and gentle when he coaxed the puppy from its hiding place, kind and gentle again when he thanked Macy and offered to drive her back to the refuge, even explain what had happened. They left quickly, Macy glancing at the bay window and saying, 'It's okay, Mr B, I don't mind, it was just an idea,' but Tillie knew that she did mind and regretted there was a new hurt where none had been before.

Susan said, 'Thank goodness for common sense.' She patted Tillie's arm, offered her a sandwich and asked about Rosie and Niko in the same offhand way that she might ask, how was your day?

Sunday–Monday and that dream, the falling one … a girl, not her, not even recognisable but still familiar, the girl on a balcony, leaning forward as if to touch the sky, the sea, and toppling, trying to fly but falling instead, oh, the rush, the terrible knowledge, the concrete closing – but then the girl jerked like a puppet and was swept upwards, the other way, past windows and balconies to the top of the building, beyond, further until she peaked, felt the hot sun on her cheeks, stretched out her arms and fell again, the rush, the knowledge –

Tillie woke early to darkness so dense that she wondered if there was anything there, beyond her. Imagine, she thought, the world rolled up and taken away like a piece of luggage while she slept … she'd open the curtains, peer out with the soft surprise with which we are tempted to greet any new day –

Nothing. A void.

Or was a void something? Like a hole – was a hole a thing? A non-thing? Life is a thing and death is a non-thing …

Awake now. She pushed away her doona. The light that filtered into her room was weak but enough for her to see her pale limbs as two branches drifting along a dark, silent river … She rotated, stood and welcomed the strength of the floor against her bare feet. Resisted the window but did open the door. Nothing there? Yes, a hallway and two doors, just as there'd always been. The family home; she couldn't remember living anywhere else.

Relief. Tillie crept into the hallway, scrunching her eyes as she passed between two mirrors, trolls at a bridge. First door, her sister's bedroom. Susan called it the spare room, probably fair enough since Rosie hadn't occupied that space for years, even though the inside was still stamped with her presence: boy-band stickers on the wardrobe, zany hat collection hanging off a rack and stuffed into drawers beneath the bed. Rosie at fifteen had defined herself with hats.

'New hat, new me!'

Little Tillie had never quite understood how that worked.

Second door, Susan and Henry's room. Did she dare? As a toddler she had been granted automatic entry, snuggling between those flubby bodies on special nights or scary nights, but that changed as she had grown. After Rosie left there'd been new space in the house, her sister's busy hands and barking voice no longer commanding immediate and total attention. For Tillie, there was no need to go into her parents' room when there were so many other places in which to play hide-and-think.

She had been about ten when that had happened, about ten and beginning to understand that everyone needs their own home within a home. Even parents.

She stood at their door and listened. Nothing. Were they there?

Listened some more. Still nothing. Irrational, but she couldn't help it … What if they're not there? What if they've gone? A holiday. Wouldn't blame them, having to share their home with a misery guts. A note pinned to the puffed-up pillow … *Sorry, sweetie, but it's just too much, you've been too much.* And Costa Rica was her mother's dream travel destination. Imagine it, Tillie! Imagine the twinkling Caribbean, imagine the forests and volcanoes, imagine seeing the quetzal bird … *sacred to the*

Maya and Aztec people, although these days the birds are often trapped or killed –

She rushed into her parents' bedroom.

Two shapes, mirrored zigzags. She could hear breathing. A murmur. One of the shapes lengthened slightly then recoiled, like a touched snail.

More light now so Tillie could see her mother's face, that button nose that Henry had always cited as the key to opening the door of his attraction – 'When you come from a family of big noses, that little cutie was always going to make something happen.' Rounded cheek, hair in unruly mounds. Susan had always struggled to control her tresses, despite the best efforts of Samantha and the Hair Today salon.

Tillie switched her gaze. Beneath the doona her father's long body was an archipelago. At the northern end his face was near submerged, the bedcover climbing his cheeks. Noticing a lick of ashen hair fallen across his eyelid, Tillie stepped forward, hesitated for a moment, then pincered the end of the hair, swung it back into place.

Now everything was as it should be, everything was in place. She sighed, edged towards the door.

'Tillie,' he murmured.

She stopped. Her father was struggling to rise.

'Tillie, love, what is it?'

'Nothing,' she whispered, 'I just –'

'Okay?'

She couldn't answer. Henry waited and eventually Tillie said, 'Couldn't sleep. Sorry.'

'Can I help? Make you a Milo?'

No, she said guiltily, no, she'd be fine, back to bed, sorry … a strange sensation, she wanted to go outside, fall on to the grass, grip the world tightly, sniff the plants and kiss the soil and be thankful that it was all there. Instead, she sat on the edge of her bed and waited for the sounds of people waking and coming out to their gardens or on to the streets, driving their cars or calling to their neighbours, normal people who didn't agonise and weren't so afraid, didn't reject gifts on the grounds of too much love, didn't endlessly de-colour themselves with sadness.

Not that anyone was giving up.

Susan drove her to yoga class on Tuesday afternoon, saying, 'Tillie, I don't mind at all – this commission is doing my head in.' She'd been asked – 'That's *asked*, no tender, so naturally I assumed they'd appreciate my ideas' – to create an installation to be placed within a windblown park on the Manly foreshore. The piece, or pieces, would symbolise the unique Australian relationship between land, people and ocean.

'Reality being, the council has no idea what they want,' Susan grumbled. 'Five designs now – five! – and it's been maybe, not sure, need to check with the stakeholders. Who? The money, that's who. Bureaucrats!'

She drove on. Mid-afternoon, the growling traffic was a pile-up waiting to happen, but that didn't stop Susan from cutting in and out, switching lanes, tailgating.

Tillie cowered behind her knees. Her mother groaned loudly and said, 'I think we just passed the turn-off. Why can't the signs be clearer? Why are people so –' She belted the car horn as another motorist refused to allow her to do a U-turn.

Yoga for Beginners was held inside a hall in Ashgrove. The instructor was a woman with sandy hair clustered into a ponytail and a newborn in a carry cot. Tillie was embarrassed to be seen in her leotard – the starkness of black material against blubbery white skin! – so she stood at the far end of the hall behind what appeared to be a parade of lithe stick insects and listened as the woman, Kristina, spoke about having an open mind and heart. Kristina put on a CD and they began, Tillie following the multitude of instructions as best she could: cross legs, roll shoulders, deep inhale and exhale, side to side, up and down, head over heart, heart over pelvis, hip over knee, shoulder over wrist, strength and softness, moving forward, moving up, moving back …

'Alignment is vital!'

That was weird. Blood was vital, water, food, oxygen – but alignment?

Chest down, bum up, chest-bum, chest-bum, Tillie thinking, what do I look like! What would the stick insects see?

Dough.

Lump.

Gargoyle.

'No need for crazy shapes in yoga,' called Kristina. 'We're not pretzels yet! And stretch … align … Relax, stretch …'

'How was that?' asked Susan. She'd been scribbling furiously in a sketch pad.

'Okay,' Tillie told her. Easy, no-quibble answer. Truth was, although she hadn't minded Kristina, Tillie didn't really see how stretching and breathing and contorting and aligning could prevent sadness.

Pointless, all of it.

Not that anyone was giving up. Macy had brought her a scrapbook of recipes for –

Positivity food?

'How can food –'

'Look at it, honey. Come on, just look.'

'It sounds weird.' As in, New Age weird.

'Will you please just look? Honestly, sometimes I wonder –'

The remainder of the sentence wedging awkwardly between them. Tillie blinked, gazed at the first recipe.

Spinach and fish pie. Without pastry.

Like algae with lumps.

'I've been researching,' said Macy with renewed vigour. 'Oh, my God, it's amazing! Truly. You need – we all need lots of Omega-3 and lots of folate. Which is an acid, which is a chemical but natural, you know, not some concoction mixed up in a Petri dish by a bunch of nerds. And this meal is perfect. Perrr-fect!'

Dutiful smile, turn the page and there was another ... turkey soup. Turkey? Stringy, tough, never liked the flavour –

'Selenium and tryptophan,' announced Macy, making the words sound like the names of friends. 'Aka, stress-busters!' She grinned and sang, 'Who you gonna call ...'

Tillie wanted to be grateful. But it's just food, she thought – we eat to stay alive, and this is –

Worthless, all of it.

Not that anyone was giving up. Her father scratched his chin and said, 'Tillie? Got a proposition for you.'

Coffee with Henry in his study while he outlined his idea, paid research. Once upon a time Henry had been an art critic for a magazine – he'd met Tillie's mother at one of her early exhibitions – then, in search of better money, a public servant with State Arts, retrenched after budget changes that he'd described as 'typical philistine stupidity'. Shoved into the limbo of forced retirement, he'd needed a project and found –

The Book.

Specifically, the Book of Bond, as in James, as in 007. Henry was compiling film data, analysis and trivia, reviews, quizzes, bios, a fan's bonanza. Q's real name? The actor who played Nick Nack in *The Man with the Golden Gun*? Most popular method of execution?

'Keeps him busy,' murmured Susan, behind closed doors. 'Won't be published though. All that stuff's online. Who needs a book?'

Don't be so smug, thought Tillie irritably. Dad needs a Book. He needs The Book.

Her father put down his coffee. He said, 'I need some help with the title songs from the films. Singers, writers and composers, lyrics, chart positions. Maybe you could do some Googling, make some notes?'

Tillie knew exactly what he was doing. This was a scheme: find an interest for his sad, uninterested daughter. Re-attach her to the world, even one that was make-believe. Get her to consider items other than herself.

However, she appreciated his kindness, wanted to at least try. That afternoon she listened to her father humming as she typed notes on Shirley Bassey, Tom Jones, Tina Turner. The information wasn't difficult to find – in fact it was very easy, an eight-year-old could –

Henry left the room momentarily. Tillie went straight to his laptop, scrolled through the manuscript – its title was 'Shaken Not Stirred' – and found chapter seven, 'The Hits'. Already the chapter was over thirty pages long, with all referencing meticulously completed.

She loved him for what he had done but it was useless, she thought, because of who she had become: sad Tillie Bassett. Sad Tillie Bassett who was destined to stay that way.

The mindfulness program was cancelled for the week, the group leader apparently suffering a migraine. Tillie, relieved, was able to return to school on the proviso that she could come home if she was 'feeling unwell'.

English, write a paragraph then write another.

Science, read a chapter then read another.

Drama, watch other people perform. 'Peer assessment,' cried Ms Andrewartha, handing out pink templates as if they were jewels.

Maths, tune in and out of an incomprehensible language.

Might well be Martian, she thought. Blended with Ancient Norse and seasoned with a pinch of Jabberwocky.

Thankful for the arrival of lunch break, she carried her sandwich to a shady, generally unpopulated part of the bottom oval – and there was Snake, waiting patiently on a bench seat. His ginger dreads seemed dreadier than ever but nothing much had changed in the rest of him: same awkwardness in the angles of his frame, same bolts of blue-green light in his eyes.

'Hey, you.'

'Hi.'

He unwrapped a muesli bar, offered her a bite. The bar was bone-dry and crumbly, Tillie wondered if it had spent last winter hibernating in Snake's bag.

'The game,' he said eventually. 'I've fixed it.'

'Didn't realise there was anything wrong.'

'Limited,' he said. 'I've added layers.'

'Cool. Layers are, you know –'

'Better, yeah. Wondering,' said Snake, 'if you'd like to give it a go sometime. When you're ready, of course. No rush.'

'Sure. Sounds good.'

They ate without further conversation as a group of Year Eights spilled like lava on to the oval and began a game of football that involved no feet, no ball and plenty of vigorous tackling.

Snake said, 'It's not my business, but –' He paused, rubbed his eyes.

'What?'

'Sorry,' he said. 'Felt a bit spaced there for a moment.'

He swigged from a water bottle then said, 'Um, yeah. Not my business –'

'It's okay,' said Tillie, thinking long-time friend, always-there friend, you can ask. You're definitely allowed.

'I guess I don't – I don't understand why you're feeling –'

Like that.

'I don't understand either,' Tillie told him. She glanced across, saw his concerned face caught sharply in the light – and the thought arose, quickly and terribly: What if Snake died? It could happen. Death didn't discriminate. Accidents, illness, freak events, cold-eyed men; death could happen to anyone. People of all ages –

Concentrate. Concentrate!

'I meant,' said Snake, 'that you don't need to feel that way. Sad and, um, alone. I – we all, you know, everyone –'

Too difficult. He drank again from his water bottle, coughed a little, then surprised Tillie by saying, 'Does it feel like you're drowning?'

'Kind of. Actually, yes.'

'I know about that,' Snake told her. 'No air. You don't just wonder where your next breath is coming from, you wonder if you even know how to breathe.'

Tillie couldn't reply. Snake coughed again before saying, 'You know Cambodia?'

'Mmm.'

'Um, I'm thinking of going there. Next summer. There's this volunteer program you can do. Building stuff for the villagers and teaching kids how to talk English, that sort of thing.'

Oh, you'd love that, Tillie thought. Go. You must go. Already she could see him sitting beneath a big-leafed tree being swamped by a horde of happy, clamouring children –

'Wondering,' said Snake.

'What?'

'If you'd maybe consider – like, think about it, but – come with me?'

April. The late sun was molten. That afternoon she'd tried Homework Club, then her mother had picked her up, spotted the Happiness Clinic and insisted that an appointment would be made, pronto.

'We're going to fix this,' she'd said.

'Mum –'

'No ifs, no buts. Tillie, everything is fixable. Everything, including this, okay? Ringing – now.'

No stopping her mother in this mood; she was an avalanche.

Now Susan was finally at the salon. Henry was visiting his friend Ralph, recovering from a hip operation, and would be home late with containers of Special Fried Rice and his usual dose of balmy goodwill.

Normal patterns, normal lives.

Tillie sat alone in the garden, surrounded by thirsty bees and colours that dripped from the flowers and soaked the earth. She closed her eyes and sent a thought out to the world.

It won't work. For all of your good intentions I thank you and love you ... but this is how I am. For now and for always.

Live as you must. Be free of me.

PART 2

His name was Gilbert and his eyes were two enormous, bobbling spheres that were close to existing outside of his face.

'Yes, I look like a goldfish.'

Tillie rapid-blinked as Gilbert said with a sense of merriment in his voice, 'You were staring at my eyes.'

'Sorry, I –'

'No need to be embarrassed, Tillie Bassett. Everyone does it, me included. With a mirror, of course. Hey, my eyes are magnificently oversized. They deserve to be stared at.'

She *was* embarrassed but managed a smile when he told her how much better the world would be, how much more enlightened, if we were allowed to gaze uninterrupted at people's various deformities – because we all have them, he said, otherwise we'd be perfect, and what or who is a perfect human? Doesn't exist, thankfully. Be grateful for the gremlins, yeah?

Tillie nodded, didn't dare do otherwise. Gilbert was kind of compelling – as long as she avoided those eyes.

'So-o-o,' he said, flicking a pen-top up and down, 'first time at the Happiness Clinic. Guessing you must be sad, right?'

'Yes.'

'Sad person who wants to be happy, haven't been that way for a while?'

She nodded again. Don't stoop to crying, she thought, not now. She glanced around. The room was spacious, naturally lit and surprisingly bare. There was a desk with a laptop, two armchairs and little else. No bookcases, no cupboards. A framed artwork was on one wall, the others left blank.

Gilbert said, 'I'm not going to ask you the reason or reasons that you're sad. I think that's a pointless question.' His tone was more matter-of-fact than critical. He said, 'If you knew there was a reason, you'd also know there was a cure. As in, I'm sad because my pet died so I need to work through my grief, maybe buy a new pet and transfer my former happiness. Or I'm sad because my life is going nowhere so I should find a new direction and give myself a chance. Most people can work these things out for themselves. They mightn't always be able to *apply* the cure but they know what it is, even if they won't acknowledge it.'

There was a scent, she realised. Citrusy? Maybe his aftershave. Smelled sharp.

'Tell me about your sadness,' said Gilbert. 'This is a *what* question, not a *why*.'

'As in?'

'What's it like?'

Tillie considered.

'Just there,' she said.

'Go on.'

'Heavy inside me,' Tillie told him. 'But I can't help it because I'm a sad person. That's who I am.'

'I see,' said Gilbert, casting away the pen and locking his fingers. 'You're a sad person.'

'Yes.'

'Genetically sad?'

'I suppose,' said Tillie; she hadn't thought of genes.

'Right,' said Gilbert, as if this was some sort of breakthrough. 'We assume genetics. That's who you are.'

She shrugged. Gilbert continued, 'Let's think about this some more. Sadness is genetic?'

'Mmm –'

'Then so too is happiness. Happy people are made that way, correct?'

This time he didn't wait for an answer. 'So sadness and happiness are genetic pals, the same as other genetic pals. The same, for example, as beauty and his or her old mate, ugliness.'

Tillie couldn't commit. Gilbert said, 'If someone is beautiful we think that they must have good genes. Lucky things, born with genes that gave them clear skin, high cheekbones and non-boggly eyes. Correspondingly, if someone is ugly then we lament their bad genes. Poor thing, copped a wham-bam from the ugly stick. So, logically, if sadness and happiness are the same, if they are as genetic as beauty and ugliness,' – he was melodramatic as he added – 'then your emotional destiny must lurk within you.'

Lurk. Like a spider.

Gilbert stood and manipulated his wrists as if he were

readying himself for a game of ping-pong.

'I can't help being sad,' he said. 'That's what you think, is it not? Can't stop myself. It's genetic therefore it's inevitable. Hey, there are plenty of highly qualified people out there who will agree with you. They'll say – dear Tillie Bassett, we accept that you are sad and what we will now do is find a cure, a drug, a therapy. We will find this cure by testing as many different possibilities as we can, until we discover the one that is most like a blanket.'

A blanket?

He manufactured the blanket with his hands as he said, 'We will mask your pain by putting our well-tested blanket over it so you don't have to see or feel or acknowledge. The sadness is not gone because that's your biology, that's your genes at work, but it is controlled. Like a smouldering fire there are no flames even though the embers remain warm. You see?'

Tillie's eyes were wide. She said, 'My doctor didn't give me drugs.'

'Glad to hear it.'

'Some sleeping pills and natural stuff, but that was all. I couldn't sleep.'

'Fair enough. Sleep is useful. Any other blankets?'

She mentioned the yoga and mindfulness classes. Gilbert left his chair, went to the wall and stared at the framed print. Tillie noticed its details for the first time: streaks and swirls of blue and green with bizarre golden creatures bobbing and hovering.

'What about this picture?' he asked. 'Do you like it?'

She did. Somehow the image managed to be both sophisticated and childlike, making her think of an older person rushing joyously into a playground; the fondly recalled promise of swings and a carousel.

'*Swimming Frogs and Dragonflies*,' Gilbert announced. 'My colleagues insisted. They said, you are operating a happiness clinic and this is obviously a happy picture so you must have it on your wall.'

'I like it –'

'I like it too but I didn't agree with their reasoning. I said, I will have this painting on my wall but not because it is happy. I will have it because it seems to me that these bedraggled creatures are *striving* to be happy, and in a purposeful manner. These bedraggled creatures understand that you cannot just leave sadness behind as if it is a cellar in an old house and you've just found a key and climbed the stairs. Nor can you find happiness simply by looking a bit harder or being lucky enough to look in the right place, like some birthday-party treasure hunt. No, first you must understand it. You must know what it is that you wish to achieve.'

He used a long index finger to trace along a vivid blue line in the painting then he said, 'Misery is easy. Nothing much involved, just wallow. But happiness? That takes effort.'

'I don't understand,' she told him.

Gilbert returned to his chair. He said, 'Tillie Bassett, you need to find out what happiness is. What is it, for others and for you? Who achieves it, and how? Make that your quest, after which –'

She waited as he opened his palms and said, 'You will have a better idea of how to reach it.'

Gilbert, she thought, made the process sound like stretching up, or flying to the moon.

Maybe it was.

'A quest?' said Susan. 'What do you mean, a quest?'

'He wants me to find out about happiness,' said Tillie.

'Find out what?' Susan sounded irritable, on edge. Perhaps, thought Tillie, her own quest was stalling, the perfect work of art beyond reach –

'Tillie?'

'Things like … when people are happy, what makes them that way.'

'Which people?'

'Anyone, I guess,' said Tillie.

Dad. Rosie. Macy. You.

'Anyone. So you're going to email the Dalai Lama?' Susan set her mouth to a frown then groaned as she saw a thick sludge of pre-Easter traffic crawling along the freeway.

'It sounds a bit San Francisco, 1960s, to me,' she said. 'Granted, only an initial consultation, but I did expect more than just – homework.'

'He was interesting,' said Tillie, feeling a sudden need to defend Gilbert the Goldfish. Who was unusual, certainly, but also – insightful? Capable of different angles?

'Interesting,' harrumphed Susan. She swerved right, earned a toot from another driver, dismissed them with a finger flick and said, 'Sweetie, given his fee I'd prefer competent over interesting any day.'

Easter Saturday they drove north to Barilba Bay. The town, arcing languidly alongside a melon-coloured coast, had always seemed to Tillie to be pale. The awnings over the shops, the greens, blues and pinks of the houses, the tired faces of the residents, the ever-receding sea, the pale sky tent-pegged over the grey beach … all faded, as if the entire place had been over-rinsed then dried by the hottest and whitest of suns. It was a very un-Susanish location but Tillie's parents were romantically attached to the town: their first holiday together had been at La Concha resort and had featured the promise of cheapie slap-up meal at a Mexican restaurant.

'Which was disastrous,' Henry said. They were driving into the outskirts, colourless paddocks giving way to Bunnings, Red Rooster, a tourist information kiosk that was closed, a Red Cross disposal store flanked by Perry's IGA.

'Yes, it was,' Susan agreed.

'I ate a raw jalapeno chili –'

'Trying to impress me, weren't you, He-man?'

'Sick for days.' He grinned. 'Fortunately, you saw the funny side.'

'I spent the weekend wandering the streets like a lost waif,' said Susan. 'At the time, there was nothing funny about that.'

Tillie had heard the story before but Macy – gifted an invitation because her father was at a conference in Sydney – Bryan was saving the world from financial ruin, she said, gotta love that guy – Macy was entranced, later telling Tillie, 'It's really cool the way your mum and dad sling off but actually adore each other.' Tillie hadn't considered that; she'd been nervous in the car, not because of her father's stoic, same-paced driving but because of the tone of her mother's ongoing criticism.

'Henry, it's called an overtaking lane … O-ver-tak-ing. You're allowed to do that, you know.'

So it was a comfort to have Macy there. Tillie, who'd only found out that morning, had been surprised but pleased. For her the Easter trip was usually about buying hippie earrings and sarongs that she'd never wear, taking sunset walks past bins made putrid by rotting fish carcasses, and eating pizza made gluggy by the inclusion of too much tinned pineapple. Mundane, but Macy's presence would undo mundane. She could make mud sparkle.

They settled into their spacious, well-appointed, faded apartment, then the girls sat on a narrow deck while Susan and Henry shopped. Macy was in wonderful-world mode: the trees over the road were gorgeous, so too the droves of whistling, chirping lorikeets; the old man selling watermelons from his flat-tray truck was cute; the scarlet hibiscus that threaded a fence line was an amazing colour; their glimpse of the tessellated sand was –

'Is that the beach?'

Tillie nodded. She said, 'It's better when the tide's in.'

'Waves?' asked Macy.

'Not really.'

'Right. Family-friendly. Guess we'll cope.'

Soon enough she forgot the beach and they focused on absorbing orange from the late sun, Tillie thinking that sitting on the deck was like being soaked in Fanta. Susan and Henry returned with chicken and chips and hired DVDs and that was the evening: curtains dancing to the tunes of the breeze, Tillie glancing occasionally at the TV screen but in reality waiting for the stars, more visible out here, to drop down and join her and Macy on the comfort of cushions.

Sadness? Yes, she thought, but distant tonight, as if resting. Like an animal, curved in a hollow.

Later, as they lay parallel in their respective beds, Macy made jokes about the lumpy mattress, the princess not finding a mere pea but a vegie patch, and Tillie actually laughed – not just at the idea of a mattress sitting on top of pumpkins and cauliflowers, but at Macy's exaggerated groan every time she shifted position. They had left the blinds raised so it felt more like camping; if she closed her eyes she could imagine the walls rippling and the ceiling shifting benignly with the wind.

Macy's sleepy voice: 'Okay, beautiful girl?'

Here, now, yes. Okay.

'Macy?'

'Mmm?'

'You're such a happy person.'

'You keep saying that.'

'It's true.'

'And I keep saying, not always.'

Really? Seems that way.

'What makes you happy?' Tillie asked. Her quest, to

find out …

'Heaps of things,' Macy murmured. Tillie heard her movement but no groan this time.

Macy's voice, when it returned, seemed softer and more distilled, like smoke on the outskirts of a fire. 'I try not to think too much about things like that,' she said. 'How I feel. I'd rather just *be*.'

The implication was clear: if you were just *being*, then all of the other possibilities, the worrying about grey hairs and vanishing geckos and cold-eyed men and girls falling from balconies, weren't happening.

Envy you that.

Tillie said, 'But how do you cope if something bad happens?'

'Like what?'

'I don't know.' She breathed deeply and said, 'What's the worst thing that ever happened to you?'

Outside: the crickets, the breeze playing piano in the trees, someone laughing. The cooling, shrinking earth.

Macy said ominously, 'Never told you, have I?'

Suddenly the air seemed very still and Tillie wanted to open the window, find the cuddle of the sea.

'I just turned up here, in Australia, and everyone assumed –'

That you were exotic. An American wildflower. Beautiful alien from a desirable world. Yes, thought Tillie, we did assume. *We* did.

'Worst thing that ever happened to me,' said Macy. 'Okay. You ready for this?'

She had to be, she knew that. 'Yes,' said Tillie.

'Definite?'

'Yes.'

Macy gave it a moment. She said, 'There was an incident at my school in Philly. Incident – stupid word. It was more than that.'

'What?'

'We were shot up by this guy in senior.'

'Shot up?'

'Yes, Tillie. Real guns, real bullets.'

Oh, God.

'I didn't know the guy,' said Macy. 'No one did. Hardly ever attended. But he seemed harmless. You know, library-monitor type.'

Her shadow arose to sit on the edge of the bed.

'One day he did turn up,' she said, 'and he had guns. Two pistols and – and a rifle. He killed a math teacher then a girl who was waiting to see the math teacher, then he went to the gym and shot at a class in there, killed some kids and hurt a bunch of others.'

Tillie couldn't move. Macy said, 'I had a friend in that class. Her name was – is – Bernie. Bernadette. She survived but she lost a leg. A fun person, Bernie. She'd been hoping for a college scholarship one day, athletics. She was a runner, very fast.'

Tillie whispered, 'Were you –'

'Next room,' said Macy. Her voice was a low strum. 'Science lab. The teacher locked the door then we sat under the desks and waited.'

Already it was one of those stories that Tillie knew she'd

never erase. There was a movie clip in her mind – the black-clad gunman stalking empty corridors, passing lockers and noticeboards, looking into the glass insets of the doors before he heard a noise, swivelled and raised his pistol –

'It was random selection,' said Macy. 'For some reason he missed us, went three doors down. Shot some more. Then the police came in and got him. Killed him, I mean. No choice there.'

Could've been you, thought Tillie. Your beautiful life, beautiful mind, Tigger cut down in an instant, no reason, no sanity.

'We survived, but it didn't just stop there,' Macy told her. 'When an *incident* like that happens, nothing can ever be normal again. You're alive but not in the same way as before. Everyone was empty. The teachers went through the motions. A few resigned, or went on leave. Kids transferred. Friends stopped being friends. People got suspicious of each other. There was lots of anger, lots of questions. Lots of what-ifs. Pretty soon I couldn't stand it any more so I left. My dad had been talking about going to Australia for work; I guess I made it a bit easier by saying that I couldn't go back, not there, not to that poor, dead school.'

Finally Tillie moved, sat alongside. She wanted to hear Macy's breathing.

'I know that I lucked-in,' Macy said. 'You want to know why I'm happy, trying to enjoy life? Because I've seen the alternative, Matilda Jane, and it sucks. Big time.'

'But why would he do that?' said Tillie. 'Why?'

She felt Macy's embrace, a soft kiss on her cheek.

'I don't know. Apparently he left some warped manifesto, conspiracy theories, hate the universe, crap like that. He was obviously a total misfit. That's the only answer to why.'

Macy straightened her back. She said, 'Whereas you, sweet girl, you are a great fit for the world. You fit much better than you realise. So maybe that's what you need to focus on, the fitting-in, the good things that can and do happen, rather than the dark possibilities. Can I give you an example?'

Please.

'Something I've been meaning to say for a while now. Which is this. Whenever I see you and old Snakey boy with your heads bent over some project, I think – well, lookee here. Look at the happy little birds that those two are.'

A shiver, a pulse.

'No,' said Tillie. 'We're just friends, we've known each other forever –'

'Doesn't matter,' Macy told her. 'I know what I see.' She lay back, laughed lightly and said, 'Hey, forget the misfits and think about this. It's okay to get to know someone better than *just friends*. It's allowed.'

Yes, but –

'We're humans, after all,' said Macy. 'We all want – we all *need* that kind of closeness. And hey, far as I can tell, you guys are part way there.'

The afternoon heat was radiant enough to melt layers. Times like this, thought Tillie drowsily, wind becomes sand, sand becomes sea. Birds might swim and fish might soar. The world is without colour, curdled cream.

They lay on the beach and basked, Macy with her ear buds in, Tillie trying not to think about the school in Philadelphia. She felt awkward and uncomfortable on the hot sand with a cotton blouse covering her head and smells in her nostrils – suncream and traces of this morning's deodorant, but also her own scent, slightly sour and lived-in.

Sensed a flop nearby, heard male voices.

'This'll do.'

She peeked through an armhole. Two boys were sitting on the edge of the dune, both clad in the uniform of cap, threadbare singlet and boardies. One of the boys, as lithe and sinewy as a dog, held a frisbee.

'Come on,' he urged.

She watched as the boys skipped and flicked, ran and caught, the frisbee a lifeline that fizzed between them. They were synchronised and remarkable, and Tillie could see that they'd been born with this: the innate knowledge of catch and throw, the reading of flight.

'Nice,' said Macy. She was sitting up, buds quickly stowed in her bag.

'Huh?'

'Those guys. Nice.'

Confident, for sure. They owned the beach. When the taller one, the dog, deliberately spun the frisbee into the bay, the other plunged into the water with a certainty that Tillie had never been able to muster or even understand. The pleasure in his shout insisted that there could be no peril – the bottom was a distance away, no rocks lurked, no creatures either.

'Cold, hey!'

'You're a wuss, mate!'

The taller boy galloped to join him and they skimmed the frisbee across the golden water, tossing up a diamond froth each time they dived and resurfaced. When they emerged from the bay, two glittery porpoises given feet, Tillie could sense something new and –

Dangerous?

'Hey,' said the first swimmer as they approached. 'How's it going?'

'Going well,' said Macy. 'How about you guys?'

The boys glanced at each other.

'American?'

'All the way, honey. You?'

Another glance, a shared secret grin.

'I'm Sean,' said the taller boy. 'This is Jed.'

Macy rose and introduced herself. She was wearing an orange bikini beneath her white top; in the sunshine and heat she blazed.

'And this is Tillie,' she said.

The boys mumbled a greeting.

'My best friend,' said Macy with such casualness that Tillie tingled. 'We do everything together.'

Which settled it. A game of frisbee with Sean and Jed …

Not surprisingly, Macy was as good as, if not better than them, oil-smooth in her athleticism.

'Sorry,' said Tillie, 'I'm not much good at sports –'

'Don't worry about it,' Jed told her. 'Just a bit of fun.'

She tried to participate, which mostly meant picking up the frisbee after it landed where she wasn't, but that was okay, not too dispiriting, and good when she did actually catch it, Jed running over to high-five.

Which settled it further. Lunch? Why not? O'Reilly's on the Nard, awesome burgers. You'd like burgers, wouldn't you, Miss America? Hot chips?

'Fries,' said Macy, twirling. The three of them laughed as one; nothing like a big wrap of chips to bring forth the stories. Tillie felt gritted, she felt burnt and ragged, but she listened attentively, the Sean-and-Jed show. Local boys, went to Holy Spirit, Sean crossing himself and laughing, hey man we're God squad, Jed suggesting it wasn't so bad, at least the teachers cared. Ish. Anyway, God was a sport and sport was the god; rugby in winter, basketball and cricket in summer, touch footy all year round plus fishing for Sean, his old man ran a trawler, whereas Jed was the brainy one, gunna be a marine biologist. Or a surfer. Gnarly dude, said Sean, no surf out there, flat as. Not like Byron, said Jed, where Dad lived – and thus came the first cloud, Jed's disappointment with his father, dislike of his stepfather. Aggro, he muttered, and a bully.

'How bad?'

'Bad enough.'

'Meet you later?' asked Sean, and straightaway Macy agreed, Tillie wondering if that meant her too, paired with Jed in the tag-along role.

'You don't mind?' They were walking back to the apartment, dodging a gambolling wind and kids on skateboards.

Tillie tightened.

Macy said, 'What? Is there a problem?'

'Macy, we don't even know them –'

'We hung out, we had lunch. Of course we know them.'

Tillie sighed. She said, 'My parents –'

'Hey, I'll square it,' Macy told her. 'Your dad won't mind because he never minds anything, and Mrs B is putty. Put-ty.'

No doubt as to what Macy wanted, thought Tillie: a cupcake version of holiday romance.

Ick.

'They're just guys,' said Macy, impatience creeping in. 'Harmless guys. Holy guys! Hey, sometimes you gotta live in the moment, okay?' Then, with an arching of the eyebrows, 'It's allowed!'

Uh-huh, thought Tillie. Go with the flow. Peace out. Chill. All those Buddhisty claims.

Still didn't feel right.

As it happened, Henry and Susan had found a new Asian–African fusion restaurant and wanted to test it, alone. Tillie wondered, when was the last time that her parents –

'Cool, Mrs B,' said Macy smoothly. 'We'll cruise downstairs for a pizza.'

'Cool,' agreed Susan. 'You cruise downstairs, get your Hawaiian Super Surprise then cruise back upstairs *straightaway*.' She added, 'Henry will pay, of course.'

They waited until the safety of sundown before meeting Sean and Jed at the band rotunda in Memorial Park. The sea breeze traced pink and blue lines in the air, and Tillie could smell sprigs of jasmine, leftover barbecue.

When Sean suggested walking to the skate bowl, she thought no, I don't want –

The flow, the flow. She stayed quiet and close behind Macy until they neared the pier and Macy darted forth, saying, let's go, it's gorgeous. Already she and Sean were swinging in and out of a private orb, giggling as they bumped shoulders and hips.

The boards of the pier creaked, old salt grinding into the sea. Sean and Macy had rattled away, so when Jed stopped to stare at the black water, Tillie had little choice but to stay with him.

It was at least peaceful. She liked the music of the ripples, the silver motes skateboarding off their crests.

'I'd like to be a fish,' Jed announced. 'Be good, wouldn't it?'

Tillie glanced at him but didn't answer. There was a lamp nearby, crazed insects batting into the white glow. Jed stuffed his hands into his pockets and said, 'I reckon if you're a fish, you don't have to think too much.'

'I guess.'

'Being a fish is uncomplicated. You swim here, you swim there. Find food, avoid becoming food. Pretty much it, hey?'

'Might be boring,' she suggested.

'Yeah, but you wouldn't know that. You're just a fish. You don't know excitement, you don't know boredom. You just know –'

Water, thought Tillie.

'Simplicity,' said Jed. 'Nothing much bugs a fish.'

A laugh bounced along the pier, dying as it fell into the sea. Tillie looked to the dark sky. She said, 'So, Sean's a funny guy?'

'Funny,' agreed Jed in his placid way. 'But not like me. Not ambitious, not interested in becoming a fish.'

It was time when nothing might become something. Macy and Sean were separated then close then separated again. Tillie thought Jed might be okay but didn't know what that might mean. When they left the pier and retraced their steps, the dull and faded town had become lively, a strip of bustling cafés and restaurants offering cut-price deals, Easter specials, free dessert, buy one get one free –

'Woh,' said Macy.

'Babe, what?'

'Tillie, look.'

She did as requested and saw her parents, seated across from each other at an outside table but leaning in, clinking wine glasses, whispering, smiling –

Kissing!

Sean was already dancing a jig, a body that needed to move.

Jed said, 'Is that your mum and dad?'

But Tillie was too entranced by their cocoon to answer. She watched as Susan pushed back and used her free hand to stroke Henry's forearm. Henry laughed and said something that made Susan tighten her grip. They sipped their wine, chewed bread slowly and stayed separate from the outer world.

'Nearly home,' said Macy cheerfully. She looped Tillie's arm and they walked, Tillie wondering what she had just witnessed. Something stronger than mere love, she thought. History channelling between her parents like a river in flood, breaking banks, unstoppable –

When they reached the apartment, Macy and Sean stepped aside to make murmurings and jab at their phones. Jed smiled before saying politely, 'Thanks for – nice to meet you.'

'You too,' said Tillie. Automatic but she sort of meant it. At least he wasn't like most of the boys at Canondale, no hungry show-off, no wolf.

'Good luck with being a fish,' she added.

Jed grinned. He said, 'Might see you in the ocean, hey?' then he and Sean disappeared quickly, as if folded into the night. Later Tillie would wonder if they had even been there, although Macy assured her that they had and it had all been fine, just a bit of fun, certainly allowable.

Back in Brisbane she endeavoured to occupy each holiday-day with a list. Her mother was straight into the studio – a break had inspired her, she said, design number six, the clincher! – and her father had fallen into one of those phases when he was only able to donate a quarter of his mind to any conversation. Regular occurrence, thought Tillie, so no point in being resentful. He did at least check on her –

'Whatcha doing today, kiddo?'

Tick the list ... Xbox, back episodes of *Gilmore Girls*, maybe write a poem, maybe screw up the poem and chuck it away, maybe listen to Adele, Xbox ...

Wait, she thought. You're fifteen. You should be living the dream – shopping online or making a blog about something that doesn't matter or uploading two hundred photos of yourself or at least sharing in the Screen Lives of Other Girls, those shiny, multi-faceted and OMG-fascinating moments when dowdy Darlenes turned into marvellous Madonnas –

No. No! Avoid logging on. Actually, avoid the world. She'd already heard the TV that morning … *synchronised bombs … a church, a marketplace … act of terror … thousands gathered in prayer … no one yet claiming responsibility …* Then, the newsreader inexplicably shifting her tone … *Australia's Easter road toll rose to seventeen last night when –*

'Tillie?'

'Read my novel for school,' she said. Which was supposed to have been done six weeks ago, the rest of the class having already begun the grim pick-apart. Venn diagram please; allies to the left, enemies to the right, the gigantism of the world reduced to opposing pairs. Was it really so simple?

Act of terror … no one yet claiming responsibility.

'Uh-huh. Good book?'

'Love story,' said Tillie.

'Is there any other kind?' Henry scratched at the side of his nose. 'Enjoy,' he said.

She took a train to a scheduled appointment and assured Dr Ev that, yes, the natural thingos, vitaminy whatever-they-weres, had helped. Okay, a lie – or was it? Maybe there had been change; she might not be aware. Might not know the signals? Anyway, she thought, it's all on the inside and that's pretty much unreadable –

As was the love story. Too much custard in the sentences and the protagonist was an over-talkative bimbo. She dropped the book into her bag, gazed out the window of the train at the usual rush-past of concrete and graffiti and found herself thinking of Macy, her school in Philadelphia. She'd said the name once … Park something. Parkside? Parkville? One of those words that would come later, three in the morning, no warning.

A church, a marketplace … a school. Around the world's orb, nowhere was safe. Poor Macy, she thought: skipped into class expecting to learn, ended up jammed beneath a desk not daring to breathe in case the killer heard. That was real fear, when the loss of the greatest gift, the only gift, teetered beyond your control. Real fear because of the cruelty of random selection – and yet here Tillie was, staring inwards at a cloggy lump of sadness and thinking it had some enormous significance. How weak she was, how trite and selfish –

Don't cry, not here. And move, it's best to keep moving. Isn't that what fish do? She jiggled her blobby knees, dragged out her phone and touched on to Wikipedia. Fish, fish … fish need to pump water over their gills to get oxygen, otherwise they'll drown. A fish can drown? What hope the rest of us? Most fish can do this themselves but some fish, like sharks, must constantly move –

Be a shark. Was that what Jed had meant? Keep moving, keep pumping water over your gills. Keep the gift going.

Snake arrived on Friday morning with perspiration on his face and an updated copy of 'Philanthropy' on his iPad. They played for an hour, Snake periodically scanning her face for approval.

'Wow,' she said. 'Amazing.'

'Really?'

'You're so clever,' she told him. 'You could –'

Hard to finish. Good old Snake, long-term friend.

Friend, she thought. It's allowed.

'What?'

'Do anything,' she said.

He reddened, closed off the game and launched into what might have been a prepared speech about Cambodia. Research: did you know, most people live in houses that are made from pieces of scrap, tiny huts, smaller than this room. Sleep on mats if they're lucky, have a mosquito net if they're really lucky. One tap in the village but even then the water isn't clean … Tillie tried hard to listen but she was drifting, not decrying his passion, but such earnestness could be difficult, like eating a big meal on a hot day … Over one-third of the people, he said, live on less than a dollar a day – one dollar! – and nearly half the children have malnutrition, and that's if they even survive, because the infant mortality rate –

Rosie, thought Tillie, I wonder if she's told Mum and Dad yet?

– not to mention the land mines, left over from the wars, and education, or lack of it … Less than half of the kids finish primary school. Less than half! So what chance have they got? What chance?

'It sounds terrible,' she said. 'Poor people. Poor country.'

'Totally.' Snake shook his ginger dreads; she almost expected them to ring like bells. 'Which is why we have to go,' he said. He paused before adding, 'It's really important.'

Tillie gazed at her space, her own laptop, her games collection, wi-fi connected speaker box, Xbox, TV, smartphone left carelessly on the floor. She said, 'You won't be happy, will you, unless you're there?' Or someplace similar, she thought, where you can be the person you were born to be.

The helper. Purposeful, noble.

Which reminded her of Gilbert and his happiness quest. After Snake had left – dog-tired, he said, sorry, don't know why – Tillie went into her father's study.

Henry listened before saying, 'The idea being, you need to understand the nature of happiness in order to better address your own – state of mind?'

She nodded.

Her father tilted his head, thought for a moment then said, 'Well, that makes sense to me. And I'm glad to help, of course I am, but I'll have to write things down, otherwise it'll just be an illogical scramble. And since we're dealing with such a big question, you might have to deal with instalments, okay?'

Tillie nodded again, remembering what Macy had said about her father, the man who never minded anything. She murmured her thanks and was near the door when Henry's voice came again, sharper than usual.

'Make sure you ask your mother,' he said. 'She deserves that much.'

But when she went to do exactly that, Susan was on her way out and insisting that Tillie accompany her; she was visiting Mrs Cooper.

'Do you good,' she said pointedly.

They took the car, which Susan had already filled with cleaning products – squeegee, bucket, two mops – two? – as well as cloths, rags and a plastic crate filled with detergents and polishes. The day was without sun or wind, the sky like shale. An overgrown hedge made Mrs Cooper's cottage difficult to see from the street. Undaunted, Susan pushed aside the gate, marched up the broken pathway, pulled out a key and unlocked the front door.

'Only me,' she called.

Inside, the house smelled like a book that is rarely opened. Mrs Cooper shuffled into the hallway, Tillie seeing red-rimmed eyes, thin bandaged legs below a shapeless shift, fingers twisted like acacia twigs as they clasped a cat with a suspicious look on its face.

'Who's that, Miss Bessie?' cooed Mrs Cooper. 'Is that Susan?'

Susan went to the older lady, gently touched her arm and stroked the cat's nose.

'How are you?'

'Can't complain,' Mrs Cooper said. 'Well, I can, but there's not much point, is there?' She laughed drily.

'None whatsoever,' Susan agreed. 'Hey, I've brought my daughter, Tillie.'

'Hallo, love. Come to help Mum?'

'She certainly has.' Susan's tone was brisk. 'Floors and

kitchen, okay?'

'Thank you, Susan. Thank you very much.'

Their cleaning was efficient, and Tillie could see that her mother relished this, a transformation for the better. Benches wiped, cups rinsed, plates stacked, floor mopped … they were all but finished when Susan left the kitchen, Tillie hearing her mother say to Mrs Cooper, 'Can I show Tillie the downstairs room?'

The answer was brief but muted. Susan returned and motioned to Tillie.

'Come on.'

The room was reached via L-shaped steps at the rear of the cottage. Susan opened the door, switched on a light and they entered together.

Tillie drew in her breath. The space was filled with paintings that shone with energy and accomplishment. She saw fields of flowers, a shimmering lake with angels overhead, bowls filled with strange, bright shapes that might have been distorted fruit, a cat nibbling on a grinning fish, a storm spinning its vortex over a harbour and dropping huge tears of silver and gold. Higher up, a prince balancing a parrot in a cage, a bridge that melted into a clock and became a bridge again, a mermaid lying alone in a crowded city street. The mermaid had a beautiful ovate face and green eyes that never left you.

'Amazing, aren't they?' Carefully, Susan lifted a painting and surveyed it before replacing the frame. 'Francine Czajka was one of the most talented artists of her time.'

'Who's that?'

'Mrs Cooper. Real name, Francine Czajka. She changed it to Cooper because it was easier for people to say and remember.'

'Mrs Cooper did these?'

'Sure did.'

'But she's blind.'

'Near-blind,' corrected Susan, 'about seventy-five, eighty per cent because of a rare cancer in her eyes contracted at the ripe old age of thirty-two. Terrible thing to happen to anyone but devastating, obviously, for a young artist. Particularly when, before that' – she gestured broadly – 'came this.'

Tillie shook her head. The story was awful, pitiful –

Random selection.

'Such talent,' said Susan in a low voice, 'laid to waste through sheer bad luck. The doctors stopped the cancer but couldn't save her vision. Francine left hospital and never painted again. Which makes you realise, doesn't it, how easy it is to lose that which we've been given?'

Overhead, the pattering of Miss Bessie, no doubt seeking her food bowl in the kitchen.

'And how important,' continued Susan, 'to cherish what we have, while we have it.'

She touched Tillie's skin on her way out, leaving her daughter alone in the middle of what was plainly a marvellous room.

Dear Tillie,

Thank you for letting me be part of your quest. I think it's a great idea and I hope that I can help you in some way.

Just to explain my 'format', I was going to do the usual thing, type this and send it via email, but then I thought no, this is personal. Whatever these are (letters, explanations — confessions?), I'd like them to be keepsakes so I've decided to handwrite on some rather nice paper that I found in the bottom drawer of my desk. Very old-fashioned, I know, but that's me!

When you asked me last week about what made me happy, I realised that I had never really asked myself that question before, not properly anyway, and I'd never talked to you or Rosie about it either. I feel guilty about that. Sometimes, it seems, the people to whom we are naturally closest aren't necessarily the people to whom we consciously reveal our inner selves. Already your project has made me think about the benefits of us being more open with each other, as a family. We have tended to be very selective about how we present ourselves. Which doesn't mean that we don't love each other because we do! We just need to get better at demonstrating that love.

Is this the time to apologise to you for not being a better, closer, more 'inner' father?

So, open-up time. I'll begin with my childhood, best

described as a silent, threatening place. I know you appreciate metaphors; think of my childhood as a desert. Deserts are quiet and empty, qualities that can equally mean peace or menace. From peace comes stability whereas from menace comes vulnerability – and that was my childhood. My desert was still and lonely, a place where terrible winds could arrive at any time, with nothing able to stop them.

I've told you before that I began life in a small town in north-eastern Victoria, Pembrooke. You also know that I was the third of four children, but outside of a few basic details, I don't think I've ever said much more than that. I haven't, for example, told you that our mother spent her days locked into a zone between fear and inertia, nor have I told you that our father's standard pattern was to adore us at sunrise and detest us by nightfall. He was a bitter, disappointed man, and I am glad that you never had to meet him.

My sisters and I understood from a very early age that we had to devise ways of either avoiding our father or not irritating him when we were forced to be in his presence. Thus, your aunt Gretel left school at a young age and found a job, eventually becoming independent enough to move to Tasmania. Our father did not trust aeroplanes and refused to fly so Gretel deliberately went to a place where it would be difficult for him to follow.

Janine was married at the age of eighteen (Peter, before Jim, a poor choice, but she was desperate to get out of Pembrooke any way that she could). Our eldest sister Carole retreated into books and never came out again. You were just four when she died. Do you remember Susan telling you that Auntie Carole had decided to live forever inside one of her books? Oddly true — before that poor Carole had become a loner whose life was defined by the characters she had read about rather than any people she might have known. Nevertheless, you would've enjoyed her company as you grew older. One of the benefits of spending your life with characters is that you at least know some interesting people and can tell a good story.

My method? At the age of eight or thereabouts I became a collector, and in this way found a kind of happiness. It all began with rocks.

Tillie, this might sound odd, but for me, at that time, rocks felt very safe. I could identify a rock and know that it would stay as it was, unchanged, forever. I liked the way that a rock stretched beyond the start and end-points of human life. Rocks, I thought, are the real deal of existence. People flit in and out of the world, thinking that we might make some sort of mark but actually huffing and puffing and blowing down as much as we build, whereas rocks remain. They just are.

I collected granite, quartzite, basalt and pumice, anything I could find to add to my collection. I cleaned my rocks, polished them, even gave them names and personalities. They became a community: the big ones in charge, the smaller ones as obedient, perfect children. I gave each rock a voice and a story, and I gave them friendships. Each morning, as soon as I woke up, I checked my collection to make sure that it hadn't vanished during the night. Each afternoon I went fossicking to find more fantastic rocks. Each night I immersed myself in the ongoing story of my community.

Back then, those rocks were the most important thing in my life. These days, even though I've long given up on rocks, I'm still a collector (hence that wall of DVDs). My life doesn't feel right, doesn't feel balanced, unless I'm collecting — and maybe having your life feel right and balanced through doing something repetitive and regular is one way that we can get closer to this thing called happiness.

Tillie, that's my first instalment ... more soon.
With much love, Dad

Three episodes of note when she returned to Canondale College: an idea, a song and a betrayal of sorts.

Ms Caruso, the Principal, welcomed back the cohort by showing slides of her Easter trip to the Holy Land: the Sea of Galilee where Jesus walked and the Dead Sea where Ms Caruso floated. No one dared to laugh at her floral swimmers or rock-ledge hips. Tillie watched briefly before becoming preoccupied with a hornet that had sneaked into the auditorium … she'd been scared of hornets as a child until Henry had told her that they were solitary creatures dedicated to nest and children. Something likeable about that –

'This is so stupid,' muttered Olivia Barker-McLeod, Tillie's right-side neighbour.

She tuned in. Allegra was at the podium while Ms Caruso stood alongside a wooden pole that had been previously concealed behind the stage curtain. There was a green-and-white-painted triangle attached to the top of the pole.

'The Friend Stop,' said Allegra in slowed-down sing-song, 'is for everyone. You're used to hailing buses? Now you can hail a friend.'

Ms Caruso extended her arm. Mr Bhandari, the Deputy Principal, trod carefully across the stage, stopped at the pole and shook hands with Ms Caruso.

'Oh – my – God,' muttered Olivia Barker-McLeod.

Allegra said, 'Thanks to the Friend Stop, you need never feel isolated again.'

She stepped back from the podium. The younger children clapped vigorously, Tillie thinking no, it doesn't work like that; you can't just pick up a friend like a takeaway. Connecting should be natural, not artificial –

'This school,' said Olivia Barker-McLeod in a much louder voice, 'is a crock.'

On Wednesday afternoon the drama class was ushered into the theatrette to view the dress rehearsal of *Godspell*. Tillie was surprised at the quality of the performance, especially that of Jesus, a Year Twelve boy-man who had the energy of a pirate and a window-rattler of a voice. But it was Simone Varela's rendition of 'By my side' that slid in the furthest, Simone singing with such poise and fragility that Tillie began to reinterpret the sounds as images – a dragonfly skimming the watery gloss, a kite dipping and rising, occasionally touching the sky.

She waited after the bell until Simone emerged from the backstage gloom.

'Simone –'

'Oh, hi, Tillie. Were you watching?'

Tillie nodded. She wanted to say wonderful-inspirational-talented-extraordinary but the words stalled and lumped like toffee in her mouth. Instead she said, 'You looked so, so –'

'Afraid?' Simone offered a thin smile, Tillie realising for the first time that the other girl wasn't pretty in any conventional sense but radiant instead, her aliveness closer to the surface than most.

'No,' said Tillie, 'not at all.'

Simone shifted her bag to her other shoulder. She said, 'Tell you a secret? I hate it.'

Hate?

'Like, I know I've got a good voice,' said Simone, 'but – this is going to sound really selfish – but sometimes I wish I didn't.'

They walked slowly towards the door. Simone said, 'It's not

so much my voice but what it brings. That expectation stuff –
you're so talented, you'll definitely make it, we envy you.'

All true –

'I'd rather be backstage.' Her laugh was hollow. 'I really
like – I love all the lighting equipment and the props, costumes,
the sound stuff. But I can't do that because, you know, there's
this – responsibility.'

To fulfil the dream?

To fulfil the dream on behalf of those who can't?

'Anyway, see you.' Simone pushed at the door, saying, 'Did
you enjoy the show?'

'Yes,' said Tillie. 'You were –'

Simone turned.

'Brave,' said Tillie.

Something to consider there, as was the message that popped
on to her laptop screen that night. *Hey, it's me, the flathead from
the north, how's things?*

'Sorry,' said Macy over the phone a short time later, 'but
Seanie gave Jed my details and he messaged me about you, and
he was very keen, persistent.'

'Even so –'

'The guy likes you! No harm in that.'

'Macy, that's my private address –'

'Well, yes, honey, no choice there because you don't use
anything public, don't ask me why.'

'You should've checked.'

'Okay, I should've checked and I am sorry but there's no damage, not really. Besides, he was at least semi-cute. You should be flattered. Or is that flatheaded?'

No damage, thought Tillie later. Not in a dramatic or significant sense, perhaps, but it was still wrong ... a friend shouldn't do that: firstly, betray your privacy, and secondly, do so in such a casual, who-cares kind of way. Unable to sleep yet again, she lay in bed and recalled a story from history – medieval times, a crack appearing in a church wall. The priest ignored the crack, saying that he was in the business of fixing souls, not bricks ... The crack widened.

Quicker than expected, the church crumbled.

On Friday night her mother suggested – insisted – that Tillie come walking with her on Sunday morning. The Ascot circuit, she said toffily, let's look at all the nice people washing their nice cars on the driveways of their nice houses that we will never be able to afford, particularly when I get sacked from this stupid commission because I can't, I just can't –

'Mum –'

'Not taking no for an answer, Tillie. But you'll need shoes.'

'I have shoes.'

'Better shoes. A proper pair of joggers with proper heel support, not those flimsy made-in-Bangladesh plimsoll things that your generation seems to find so beguiling.'

No response needed to that!

Susan shook her head, made a bit-the-lemon face. She said, 'Tomorrow I have *another* meeting with the bureaucrats. On a

Saturday, ridiculous! Anyway, I can drop you at Westfield on the way.'

Which wasn't so bad, in fact the anonymity available within a large shopping centre could even be regarded as welcome. Tillie meandered past all the fashionable clothes shops – did women really pay so much for so little? – to the shoe store. Her mother had given her a discount voucher. She bought a pair of anonymous white joggers with proper heel support and *outstanding* arch support then celebrated by weaving into the food court, indulging in a slushy and sitting in a corner to sip and observe.

A girl in a neat brown uniform, holding a tray of coffees, hurrying by.

A mother with two chubby kids, the family stuffing themselves with tacos and burritos, *and* a plate of chips coated in tomato sauce *and* Cokes all round. Tillie checked her phone … it was nine-thirty.

Two men in suits, hurrying by. A third man, following, gesturing.

A group of finely dressed ladies merging, air-kissing then setting forth with the nicely dis continuation of employers in a foreign land.

Three girls, each shoulder-carrying multiple bags, each jabbing at her phone as they hurried by.

An older couple holding hands and bending to peer into the shopfront windows, taking it slow, one by one, a week's work here.

Individuals and groups, isolated but also included, all part of the shopping-centre gang on a Saturday morning. Was this the secret, she wondered? To shop, chat, eat and drink, pick up a bargain, lay-by a treat … to participate in the simple buy-and-sell of life?

Rosie touched her scar then took her finger away quickly, as if the flesh was red-hot. She grimaced and said, 'I know, I'm a terrible daughter. Niko is always saying …' Her voice trailed away. Tillie and Rosie were outside in the garden, could've been small children as they settled cross-legged near a hedge. Susan was out, negotiating exhibition space with a new gallery – Rosie wouldn't have been there otherwise – and Henry was brewing coffee.

Rosie said, 'I know I'm being stupid but I just don't want to deal with the reaction. No, qualify that … I don't want to deal with *her* reaction.'

'She'll be fine,' Tillie suggested, but Rosie was not convinced; it'll become *her* event, she said, *her* life as a doting grandma rather than the baby, or me. Certainly not me. It's always been about her, don't you think? She'll want to tell me how to raise it: breast milk not formula, let-it-cry, she'll probably even want to name it. Tillie didn't agree, but Rosie was acute edges and hard, ringing surfaces today, not inclined to blunt or soften, so Tillie said nothing and they moved on to a related matter, Rosie's teenage diary.

'I've never done this before, MooMoo. Never shown anyone this wacko little book.'

'Not even Niko?'

She laughed. 'Especially not Niko! Can't have my husband-to-be thinking that he's marrying a nutcase.'

Tillie said, 'You're not a nutcase.'

'Not now,' conceded Rosie. 'But I was close.'

Rosie's contention was this: she'd been deeply unhappy as a child because of her combative relationship with Susan. The latter hadn't changed, however –

'Now I'm very happy,' said Rosie. 'At least I think I am, which is what matters. And that's my point, MooMoo. Read this angry diatribe and you'll wonder how on earth the author came to be the stable, loving creature that she is now. But it does happen. It does. In my case, I was able to let go of the dismal past because I happened to find the right person to take me into a beautiful future.'

Don't want to deal with her reaction … Tillie wondered if Rosie had truly let go of the past.

They both heard it, Henry's call that coffee was ready. Rosie hunched forward, tapped the diary. She said, 'I worked out eventually that I'd been somehow born into the wrong space, so I had to leave that space and find somewhere else.'

To be happy. The diary was expensive-looking, leather-bound, with a tarnished metal clasp. Rosie rubbed its covers before handing it to Tillie.

'Nothing but the best container,' she said, 'for my vicious, unholy thoughts.'

That night, Tillie began to read:

I am writting this because one day it will be published and THE WHOLE WORLD will know how much my life SUX! I am a prisoner in this house that I HATE. Today I was locked up forever for questioning. Which is dumb because isn't that what I'm supposed to do, question? How else will I know something? Oh sorry dam that was another question. So this is how it goes, if I don't ask a question then I'm lazy and uninterested and if I do then I'm mouthy and impertinant so I don't win no matter what. Talk when I want you to talk and the rest of the time you can shut up and get back in your box, prisoner number 1234 from cell number 5678.

Later:

JS has invited me to his BP and I really want to go cause it's JS hot hot hot but she'll say no because that's her specialty that's her gift to the world, saying no and therefor hurting me not to mention everyone else who unfortunatly meets her. Really cool specialty, hurting people. And she'll come up with some crap like your turn to babysit T and he'll agree because that's what he does its probly easier and takes him out of the firing line but some support would be good? A change that's for sure. He's such an old pillow and I might even love him but sometimes I wish. I wish! The party's tomorrow nite and I HAVE TO GO everyone else is and they just got a general invite but JS asked me personally me me me! Yay!

SOOOO EXCITED and gotta go no matter what so time for Plan A Plan B and every other mad Plan ever invented C D E F G and Z. She can't say no if she doesn't know! (My new slogan).

Followed by:

So unfair. HATE her. HATE HATE HATE!!!!!

Hate Poem

I hate you because you knew I was going
And pretended to let me go
So you could follow me
And embarass me
And hurt me (again)
This time in front of my friend
Which is unforgivable
You tried to pretend that you were worried
But that's a big fat lie
From a big fat liar
And that's also why I hate you
Because one minute you lie
And next minute you tell me that it's bad
to lie.
Hypocritt!

Tillie was waiting for Snake to come around so they could test each other on the periodic table when her phone trilled, and it was Gilbert.

'Tillie Bassett, check-in call. How's the research going?'

Underway. Although Rosie's diary … like biting into what looks like cooked meat and finding it raw and bloody.

'Going okay,' she said.

'Thoughts?'

Not yet. Fresh bubbles, forming, floating.

'Too early,' she said.

'Fair enough. Hey, got a quote for you. You like quotes? My belief, there's infinitely more value in a decent quote than a pack of tablets, chemical or otherwise. You ready to record? Laptop primed, or are you a parchment-and-quill type? Actually, I think you might be.'

'Ready.' Why did this unusual man make her smile so easily?

Gilbert said, 'Guy called George Santayana, a philosopher. Dangerous profession, that. Anyway, Santayana said that "knowledge of what is possible is the beginning of happiness". Shall I repeat?'

He did so anyway. Tillie thanked him and Gilbert told her that was fine and dandy, be good to see her again, maybe next week, he had appointment-space on Thursday.

'Have a think about that quote,' he said. 'Georgie-boy was big on getting ourselves in tune with the world *as it exists*. As in, there's already a whole raft of stuff in place; our job is to fit in with what's there and use that stuff to seek opportunities. Do that and happiness may well follow.' Gilbert coughed and continued, 'Not surprisingly, he wasn't so big on religion – hope I'm not offending here – because he believed in the natural, not the supernatural.'

Tillie had made a practice of avoiding the God question

because of its abnormal size and weight, but that was like trying to sidestep your own shadow … She was writing furiously as Gilbert said, 'Hey, good talking to you, Tillie B. Hope to see you next week.'

Still writing furiously when the house phone rang. Tillie heard Henry pick up, a series of murmurs then his clarion call, 'Tillie. Come here, please.'

He was waiting in the lounge room, phone extended.

'For you,' he said; there was a curiosity in his face. She took the phone.

'Tillie? It's Carmel – Mrs Connors.'

'Oh, hi, Mrs –'

'I wanted you to know,' said Snake's mother in a rush, 'that Felix has been taken to hospital.'

Tillie had felt sick at the news, scooped out by a cold spoon. They waited in the hospital's lounge area and it took her what seemed like a long time to realise that Henry was holding her shoulders, maybe steering, maybe just holding.

'Why can't I see him?' she cried, and her father tightened his grip, murmured something.

Ticking and shuffling. Distant voices, hushed with self-importance. That too-clean smell, overpowering.

Doors that refused to open.

Finally, a nurse glided smoothly across the carpet and said that they were fine to go through.

Inside Ward 15B the TV was off and Snake was lying as if butterfly-pinned to the tight white bed.

'It's nothing,' he said.

But he was as pale as the sheet that covered him.

'I got dizzy,' he said. 'I fell.'

Like a stone. Carmel Connors told her version of the story: Felix was mowing the lawn as always since his useless father had taken off with Madam – nearly three years ago! How time flies! Carmel had been watching, thinking what a good boy he was, her eldest son, always kind, always helping out with the chores and the littlies … There was an odd moment, Felix's arms splaying like he was trying to balance on a tightrope before he wobbled and dropped.

Like a stone.

'Fainted,' she said. 'That's what I thought.'

Until the ambos checked his vitals and found a heart hammering into overdrive.

'He's okay now,' Mrs Connors told herself, but Tillie could see the pain brooding beneath a mother's skin. Carmel Connors didn't just love Snake, she needed him. He was the stillness and core; he held the spokes in place.

Snake gazed at the ceiling.

'It's nothing,' he said again, but it was *something*, they all knew that. The doctors were planning tests.

Tillie, cowering at the side of the room, had no idea what to say. Her conversations with Snake had always been intersecting creeks, the water flowing beneath a soft balletic light. Now she felt tongue-tied, her words no more useful or accessible than the grim pebbles that sat beneath the water.

Eventually she said, 'Macy said to get well soon,' which was a lie but not a bad one. Macy would have said get well soon if she'd known that Snake had dropped like a stone, in fact she'd be here now, brightening this tepid little cell with her energetic snap – whereas all she, Tillie, could do was hang around like a useless bystander and have no words.

'We should go,' said Henry eventually. 'Tillie, how about we come back tomorrow? Would that be okay with you, Felix? Mrs Connors?'

Yes, of course, thank you, thank you for … Suddenly they were in the corridor, carpark, car, and Tillie was crying small insistent tears, her father not bothering to offer the usual semi-formed soothers, instead massaging her hot silly head and letting her squeak and snuffle and expel. Please, she thought, Snake has to be okay. There's so much he needs to do, more than anyone … God, if you are there, please don't take him. It's not right, never right, to take the pure-hearted.

But later she couldn't stop the terrible thought: that of a world without her friend, a grey and terrible world where the dust would smother everything, a wasteland into which you might wander in search of a flicker, a voice or an eye, bruise or tear, scrap of flesh, speck of blood – but the cold ash would be thick and unforgiving.

She lay in bed, a drumbeat in her skull. No. No, no, no!
No! Please …

Finally the morning light, vague and ice-coloured. Tillie was a scrap – no blood, no shape. Somehow she made it to the kitchen, watched her mother drink tea, eat a banana, tap a tune impatiently on the bench.

Susan said, 'Tillie, I feel like painting. You want to paint?'

No choice once she saw the studio, her mother having already set up paper on easels and loaded an octagonal table with brushes in jars, tubes of acrylic, palettes to dab and mix.

'What am I supposed to paint?'

Tillie's small, plain, don't-want-this voice.

'Just brush strokes,' said Susan lightly. 'Vary the colours. See what forms.'

Well. Dumb. Of course nothing would form … nothing worthwhile, nothing that she could perceive.

Anyway –

It was, admittedly, good to stop thinking in lieu of stroking and slashing and carving and squiggling, her only goal being to make the nothing into a better looking nothing that she could at least abide. Meaning colour …

And shape, texture …

Meaning this weird identity-thing beginning to happen … Somehow, her nothing had become something.

'That looks promising,' said Susan.

No.

No, still an unrecognisable blah-blob … Maybe, she thought, I can pretend that it's abstract or expressionist and say, this is how I feel. This is how I am! This part is fear, this is anger, this is uncertainty, this is what happens when the dust coats my heart and this, this –

She glanced across. Of course, her mother's art was golden, tilting towards glorious. Tillie shoved the wet brush into a jar and said abruptly, 'Mum, why do you do this?'

'Do what, sweetie?'

'Make stuff,' said Tillie, knowing how resentful she sounded but that was apt enough because she *was* resentful – towards herself for agreeing to squeeze out the blah-blob while her mother did as she always did, created in a dazzling though still concrete and useful way, her mother who was able to exist so vividly and potently by bringing works of intricate beauty and consideration into the world for people to desire ... How lucky, thought Tillie, to be in love with the making of things that others will also love.

Susan stepped back. She said, 'Why do I make stuff? Tillie, because I need to.'

But it's just art. No one needs –

'Stops me from falling,' said Susan.

Her indomitable, care-not-a-whit, mad-haired mother? Briefest thought: a girl, a balcony. The rush, the knowledge ...

'Back into the abyss.' Susan rubbed her forehead as if to wipe clear her mind then lifted her brush and steadily dabbed. A wing became more defined, a cloud gathered silver threads. She said to Tillie, 'There's a lot of pressure, isn't there? To be able to *do something*. You're good at whatever, you should do that. For the rest of your life – do it, be good at it and you'll be automatically happy. Is that the message from school? Find something you're good at and you'll be fine?'

'Sort of,' said Tillie. Yes. Yes!

'I'm sure they mean well,' her mother suggested, 'but in my experience, that kind of approach is off the mark.'

Now the resentment was fading and Tillie did want to listen. Susan waved vaguely at the cluttered walls and shelves of the studio and said, 'The thing is, doing all this, making stuff as you put it, doesn't necessarily make me a happier person. I'll admit, there are times when it's utter bliss but at other times it can be torture. So much blankness, so much self-doubt.'

'Then why?' asked Tillie.

'Like I said, compelled,' Susan told her. She put down her brush. 'For me, this is like oxygen. It's not a matter of liking or disliking what I do but knowing that I need it, like I need oxygen. I need my art to live.'

She considered a moment longer then said, 'To rise. To thrive.'

Wow.

'It's that important,' sighed Susan. 'Although not as much as –'

Say it, thought Tillie. Please.

'You. Rosie. Henry.'

Somehow they'd fallen into an embrace, Tillie thinking obliquely that her mother had always used one perfume, the scent as much a part of her as if the womb that had long ago carried her tiny form had also carried this scent.

Tillie could hear the beginnings of rain tip-tapping on the roof.

'Mum?'

'Mmm?'

'What did you mean before, when you said that being good at something isn't necessarily the answer?'

Susan disengaged but stayed with Tillie's hands. She said,

'Do you know what I most love to do?'

'Make your art –'

'No, that's compulsion. This is love. Cooking, Tillie. I love to cook.'

Instant visions: scrambled eggs with dark crusts, the legendary casserole that morphed into a lumpy tomato soup, experimental scones turned on a rack like rocks, blackened sausages with mushy spines –

'Oh, I know,' said Susan with a groan, 'I'm terrible at it. Terrible! I have all these ideas and get distracted so your father has to step in – he's so careful and precise – but Tillie, I still love it! I mess up, but so what? I mightn't be able to cook but I still love to try. Even if you and your father would prefer otherwise.'

'So you're saying, it's good to mess up?'

'Not good but certainly acceptable! Sweetie, if I was a perfect cook I'd give it up and try something else. What do they say? If you can't *im*prove then you've nothing *to* prove.'

Second wow.

'Imperfection is a gift.' Susan's smile was childlike as she added, 'I ought to know. I live with it every day.'

Outside the rain was so thick and green it could've been grass that fell and settled on the ground before rising with the new day. Tillie appreciated how the rainfall muffled other sounds in their world. House-groans became murmurs. Nearby traffic might have rerouted to distant roads while planes lifted to a higher part of the sky, a blue aquarium beyond the green.

Even her thoughts were softened, her mind closing its pores

and resting like an anemone on the tideless bed of the ocean.

She didn't hear the phone but her mother brought the handset to her. Mrs Connors again. He's home tomorrow, she said. Testing is done. He's better by the minute, he'll be fine, he really will. Tillie, would you like to come over? I know Felix would love to see you.

'Just you,' she said. 'He doesn't mention anyone else.'

That night, the rain still gently roaring, Tillie sent a text to Rosie.

Who was JS?

Rosie's reply: *Ha! Old flame, Jack Savage. Thought I was in love.*

Tillie: *But not really?*

Rosie: *Nah. Jack was a Bad Boy. That was the attraction. We got together for a while but I knew straightaway it was a mistake, wrong.*

Tillie typed: *Why did you get* – then stopped because she already knew Rosie's answer. To locate a reputation and wear it like a coat. To be someone, even if that someone was wrong or misguided, because any label was better than anonymity.

Better than being Susan Bassett's daughter.

She deleted *Why did you get* and wrote: *Thanks for letting me read your diary.*

Rosie: *No probs* – followed by an old joke: *Love you to the MooMoon and back.*

More rain. For once, the prospect of a deep and gentle sleep. Her last thought: all these blessings in a single day.

Dear Tillie,

Time for part two. Sorry it's taken a while but I want to get this right. It's important for both of us.

As you know, I was a collector of rocks – until the day I arrived home from school and my collection was gone. The cardboard containers were empty. Some had been ripped apart. Not a rock in sight. None in the other rooms, in the yard or on the street. I was devastated.

My father was waiting in the kitchen. He told me that I didn't need any rocks because there were enough in my head. He thought this was very funny. He said it over and over while my mother went to a different room.

'Rocks in your head, boy, and no room for anything else.'

Tillie, I tried to hit him, something I had never done before and have never done to anyone since. Of course, it was a stupid and ultimately painful course of action. He was a very physical, powerful man.

A better idea, I decided later, was to find something new to collect, but in a way that could be secret. I had thought that my father would leave my collection alone; I was wrong.

At that time, boys in our town were expected to play sport for the local Pembrooke teams, football in winter and cricket in summer. Whether or not you liked football and cricket was irrelevant; you had to play. Pembrooke is the kind of town where Jonesy plays ruck for the Panthers just as his father Old Jonesy did and his father Even Older Jonesy before that.

My father had played and been pretty good too. There were boards in the clubrooms with his name written in gold: Best and Fairest, Club Captain, Leading Goalkicker. Whenever I was there, the blokes around the club used to say, 'Here's Henry, chip off the old block.'

But I wasn't. Footy was manageable because I could stay on the edge of the ground and not cause too much damage. But cricket — Tillie, you won't be surprised to know that I was hopeless. Zero coordination, less skill. But the unwritten rule, and my father's legacy, meant that I had to bumble along each summer being named and shamed — until a new coach came along, a schoolteacher by the name of John Davey. John took one look at my batting and bowling and rather than belittle me, or try to make me into the cricketer I was never going to be, he asked me to be the team scorer.

It was a role that suited me perfectly. The scorer is always involved in the game, there's counting and symbols, neatness, patterns — and statistics. Cricket is a game with a zillion stats, and I was happy to collect as many as I could. Pretty soon I was the cricket-stats whiz, a role that made me very happy. Rather than being the useless sod who couldn't play I was the bloke with the data: the season's averages, best scores, win-loss records. For this, I was valued.

Tillie, away from the scorebook I never wrote any of these statistics down, my logic being that if the collection stayed in my mind then my father couldn't destroy it – unless he destroyed me as well.

I've been collecting ever since. At the moment, it's the James Bond stuff. Three years ago I joined the International Cloud Appreciation Society in order to collect and understand cloud patterns (I've never told this to anyone else, not even Susan). Here's a funny one: for the four years that I was at university I collected all of my bus, tram and train tickets and glued them into a scrapbook. I'd sit in my room – I lived in a boarding-house at Caulfield – and look at my ticket collection and try to remember each journey: where I'd gone, what I'd seen, and how that particular time of my life had worked out.

Tillie, no doubt my collections point to an obsessive nature and a need for security. But they might also suggest something about our search for happiness – that we each must find a part of us that can be fed and honoured without too much mess or pain, and focus our identity on that part.

That's it for part two. Now I need time to think about my next instalment, which will be about my best, favourite and longest lasting collection.

I hope that all this is helping (somehow) with
your quest.

With much love, Dad

They were paired in history, the task being to prepare a SlideShare on Australia's commitment to the Vietnam War.

'My pop went to Vietnam,' said Macy. She was restless and out of rhythm, had already, uncharacteristically, refused to contribute. 'You do it,' she'd said, 'I don't care.' She drummed two pencils hard enough to irritate the pair of geeks at the next desk. 'He was drafted and went but he doesn't talk about it. Not ever.'

Tillie offered a vague nod. Back at school more days than not, she'd been rocked when her history teacher, Mr Wiley, had suggested that her recent *prolific* absences had sent her usual B plummeting towards the overcrowded plaza of mid-to-high Cs.

'Sir,' she'd said, 'I couldn't help being away,' to which Mr Wiley had replied, too snootily she'd thought, 'Well, I can't mark what I haven't got.'

No joy there, meaning that it was time to focus. Tillie siphoned various black-and-white images on her laptop. A fleet of helicopters flew low to the ground, raptors seeking their prey. A wide-eyed soldier tiptoed through dense jungle. Long-haired men stood beneath a banner: *Resist the Draft, Don't Register.* A naked child screamed as she ran down a road, smoke billowing behind her.

'Poor old Pop,' said Macy. There was an unusual edge

to her tone. 'He must've seen some horrible things. All that destruction and killing. Murder by Agent Orange. Can hardly blame him for refusing to talk about it.'

Tillie murmured her agreement, clipped a photo and dropped it into the SlideShare.

'He's entitled to his silence,' said Macy, 'because war's real, isn't it? *Real* trauma, as opposed to pretend.'

Tillie looked up. Macy's face was flushed. She was leaning against her chair, legs up, elbows jutting. Tillie glanced around, saw Mr Wiley in the farthest corner with Demi LaRoux and Oscar Norton, his obvious favourites, Demi with her endless questioning – 'But why, Mr Wiley, why?' – and oddbod Oscar with his knitted monobrow and non-fiction reading habit. They were an enclave of three, cheerfully splicing and dicing the history of the world.

'Sorry,' said Tillie, 'to hear about your pop.' Back to the project, clip-drop, clip-drop.

'Real trauma,' said Macy again. Then, unexpectedly, 'Heard from Jed?'

Tillie felt her own face flush. Given the circumstances it was a topic to avoid – more so since Jed had actually been in contact, sending her images of cartoon fish doing un-fishy things like chilling on beach lounges or fishing a lake filled with people. The images were cute and quirky and she'd liked them, but not replied.

On principle. Clip-drop.

'I think,' said Macy, leaning forward, speaking softly, 'that it's time.'

Sudden chill.

'Time for what?' muttered Tillie.

'Time for you to snap out of this – whatever you're in. Snap out of this place where you make a big deal about me giving Jed some basic information –'

'Macy, I'm sorry, but it was wrong and you don't seem to realise how –'

'Tillie, I have apologised. Or doesn't that count any more?'

'Of course it counts –'

'Doesn't seem that way, given the Big Freeze. Hey, while you're at it, snap out of this other place where you keep making an even bigger deal about feeling a bit dejected. Like no one else has ever felt that way –'

'A bit dejected?'

'Uh-huh.'

Tillie said, 'You don't believe me?'

'Doesn't matter what I believe. I'm just saying it's time, you know. We get it. You don't feel so good. Well, that happens.'

Yes it does, and –

'And people get over it,' said Macy. 'Like you need to.'

Her mind was popping. Get over it? Did Macy really say that?

'It's not that easy,' said Tillie. She heard her voice break like a wave, the wash spreading thin and soaking rapidly into the sand.

'Whatever,' said Macy, 'what-ever.' She pulled her books into a pile. 'This stupid quest thing. You want to know what makes people happy? I'll tell you. Being grateful. That's the secret, okay? You want to be happy, then learn be grateful.'

'I am –'

'For a whole bunch of things,' Macy told her, 'that you just keep refusing to see.'

'Macy, that's not –'

'No,' said Macy, 'no. Heard enough. Sick of it.' She picked up her books and pencil case, lifted herself like a disturbed bird and said, 'By the way, I've got my own *quest*. Something to make me happy, which you seem to think is my permanent state of being, which shows how little you actually know.'

How little you actually tell me –

'And I was going to let you in on it because I thought you'd be interested and might even want to join me, but now I'm kinda reconsidering because it seems at the moment that you wouldn't care a damn about me or anyone else for that matter, so why bother?'

Tillie, pricked by tears, didn't answer but the thought pounded: you offer me cures like a dog and recipes – a boyfriend! – and assume that's it, the world is tilted back on to the correct axis. You think that's all it takes?

'Uh huh,' said Macy again. Then, more devastatingly, 'Say nothing, Matilda Jane. It's what you do best.'

She walked away, Tillie hearing her call in cool, dulcet tones, 'Mr Wiley, did I tell you about my pop? Thing is, he was at Vietnam.'

'Niko wants to send you something,' Rosie said over the phone. 'For your quest. It's awesome. You'll like it a lot.'

Tillie thanked her. When Rosie said that was fine then immediately asked what was up, Tillie told her, Macy's criticism had left her broken and hollowed.

'It'll pass,' said Rosie. 'If she's truly your friend …'

Tacit agreement; sometimes matters of truth were best left alone. They retreated into safe zones, Rosie revealing that she and Niko had discussed buying cows.

'We want to make our own cheese,' she said, 'but after the baby, of course, need to get used to the new routines –'

'Rosie?'

'What?'

'Have you told them?'

A pause before Rosie said, 'Sort of.'

Tillie waited.

'I told Dad,' said Rosie, her voice diluting. 'And I asked him to tell Mum.'

'What did he say?'

'MooMoo, it was lovely. He was really excited.'

'Rosie, what did he say about telling Mum?'

A second, longer pause.

'He said no,' said Rosie. 'Said it was up to me. Look, I'll figure it out. Check your email, okay? It'll come as a link.'

She checked an hour later and discovered a link that led to a video clip: Niko leaning against a fence post on the western fringe of the farm, close by the disused barn. He waved and said, *Hi, Tillie. I was thinking about your quest to find out what makes people happy, and I thought I'd like to give my point of view. Hope that's okay!*

She smiled: Niko eased off the fence and glanced at the sun-dappled paddocks and the purple ranges as the camera zoomed in to his broad, stubbly face.

For me, it's really important to know where you've come from and what you belong to. Over time I've come to realise that my personal happiness is connected to how close I am to the people and places that I love. My grandfather was and still is a very big part of this. I've already told you a little bit about Grandpa; now I'd like to tell you some more.

The image faded, morphing into a still shot of an island, unfamiliar. As Niko spoke, new images emerged and disappeared: a statue of a beautiful man, a harbour filled with boats, another man with a long beard and a proud look on his face as he held up an octopus, a black-clad family with a baby in swaddling, soldiers scrambling down a snowy slope, a group of smiling women with spades and axes, buildings – broken and smouldering, two men with their arms over each other's shoulders standing near a line of small, wind-shaped trees, a wooden boat set low in the water, grim-looking people huddling in a room, a man in uniform and, finally, what looked to be a village with white houses, white streets and a brilliant blue sky overhead.

Niko said:

This is Naxos, where my grandfather was born. It's an island in the Mediterranean, a beautiful place. They say that on Naxos the god Zeus spent his childhood in a cave and the princess Ariadne married the god Dionysus. There's a quarry that supplied the marble for the great artist Michelangelo and a deep harbour for the fishermen. Plenty of fish in Naxos; the octopus is particularly sweet and valued.

That's my grandpa. Before he came to Australia Grandpa lived in a village called Moni, set into a hollow in the centre of the island. I went there once, not long after he passed away. Moni is very traditional. There are olive groves and old men playing with their beads and rocky slopes for the goats. If you climb the slopes, you see the ocean.

As a child, one of four, Grandpa helped with the vegetable garden. His father made olive oil, using a press. His mother cooked and sewed and gossiped with the other mothers of Moni. Theirs was a simple, predictable life.

Late in 1941, during the Second World War, when my grandfather was thirteen years old, the Italian army invaded Naxos. They wanted to rest their troops and plan their strategies. The Italians took over the gardens, the farms and orchards. They forced the islanders to give all of their food to the soldiers. Little matter that the islanders would starve – the stomachs of the Italian army were far more important!

The islanders were naturally upset by this but decided that the best course of action would be to secretly grow other crops elsewhere. In the meantime, there were fruit and nuts in the forests and wild animals, such as pigs and goats, to kill and eat. They would survive until the next crop.

When the Italian army realised what the islanders were doing, they decided that this was a form of rebellion. Secretly grow crops on their own island – how dare they! So the Italians spied on the villagers, followed them and destroyed the new crops. On their way back to the villages, they destroyed the olive orchards then they destroyed the homes of those who had rebelled. Any islander who protested against this vandalism was beaten up or even killed.

By mid-1942, the people of Naxos had lost their crops, their homes and, in some cases, their lives. What now? Would the survivors take to their boats and flee? Sit amid ruins and starve? Perhaps they would fall at the feet of the Italian army and beg?

None of those. As the Italians continued to wage war, the islanders began to quietly rebuild their homes, reseed their farms and gardens, and replant their orchards. If the Italians knocked down the rebuilt home or destroyed the new farm, then the islanders simply waited a month or two before starting again.

Eventually the Italian army had to leave Naxos. The islanders no doubt breathed a huge sigh of relief. However, not long after the Italians left, the Germans arrived. They too wanted to occupy the island but they were even crueller and more violent than the Italians. They torpedoed the caïques, the traditional boats, so that the islanders could not go out and fish. They destroyed the new farms and orchards and blocked all food supplies to the island except their own, thus causing what became known as the Great Famine.

Despite this, the people of Naxos refused to bend or be destroyed. Their response to the German occupation was to organise a Resistance force to find ways of sabotaging the Germans. This was dangerous work, of course. Anyone who *was identified as Resistance was tortured or killed.*

My grandfather, fifteen at the time, was a Resistance fighter. He was a small person, very fit and able to creep into a munitions depot and plant a bomb, or swim through caves to a point beneath a German lookout and plant another bomb. He was incredibly brave and loyal to his island.

Finally, late in 1944, under pressure from the Allied forces and the Resistance, the Germans were forced to evacuate Naxos. Did the people rejoice? Of course. Did they vow revenge? No. They were more interested in freeing prisoners and returning to their villages – to rebuild their homes, reseed their farms and replant their orchards. Which was exactly what they did.

The final still-image vanished and there was Niko again, gazing out at the land as he spoke. There were spaces between his words and sentences, and she could hear that distinctive country hum, life evolving without pause inside the earth and grass, the trees, rivers and sky.

Tillie, I'm a better and happier person for knowing the story of my family. It's really important for me to remember that I come from people and a place with strong values, and to understand the necessity of always seeking to rebuild, reseed and replant. My goal is to always remain true to those values. I am happiest when I do this well.

I hope you've enjoyed the story of my grandpa and our heritage. Let me know if you'd like to talk some more.

That wave, again, then –

Love you Tillie.

Tillie had visited Snake's house a few times, and remembered it as one of those shapeless, haphazard places with lots of rooms, and lots of children flowing in and out of those rooms.

Carmel Connors was late to the door so Petey opened it; he'd grown since last time but maintained the wild-eyed energy that meant he had to always be first. First up in the morning, first in every race, first to the door.

'Fe-lix! It's your girl-friend!'

'Oh, Petey,' said his mother, 'go now. Go!' She ushered Tillie away from Petey's sniggering into another room, apologising as they went. 'He has no manners,' she said, before adding, 'Boys of that age need their dad.'

Snake was sprawled across a couch, laptop balanced on his knee.

'Hey, you!'

He moved over and Tillie sat down. The room, unofficially converted by Snake into his personal retreat, was a mess of computer equipment, sketch pads, techie books, consoles and monitors, games in lidless plastic boxes or spilled across the floor, magazines, speakers, cords and power boards. There was a small round table bearing a wood-carved miniature of Rodin's *The Thinker* that Tillie had bought last year at Riverside Markets for Snake's birthday. The door was still open so they could hear the other children at play: Petey goading, Merreline squealing, Jasper's high-pitched laugh, Lizzie building her wail into a fully calibrated scream.

'I'll go,' said Snake.

'No.' His mother's smile was tired but firm. 'You have a

guest. Leave them to me.'

She marched out, closing the door on the way.

'Well,' said Tillie.

'Yeah.'

'How are you?'

'I have a syndrome,' Snake told her.

A lurch within, but Snake grinned an apology and said, 'It's okay, syndromes are okay. Much better than diseases. Syndromes have been studied and identified. They've got proper experts and titles. When you have a syndrome, it's like joining a club.'

His tone was lightweight, Tillie not sure whether he was convincing her or himself.

'What syndrome?' she asked, and this time Snake answered with what sounded like a prepared speech … His condition had been identified as Wolff-Parkinson-White syndrome, one person per thousand, overly fast heartbeat, loss of breath, dizziness, fainting.

'Tachycardia,' he said.

'What's that?'

'Technical term for a heart that goes gangbusters.'

The speech continued: usually people have one cable in their heart, we Wolffies have two, thus causing the extra load. Tachycardia is like too much electricity. Tillie didn't really understand, but she was relieved when Snake said that he was fine; he'd been given some tablets and the syndrome was treatable, if needed, through a simple procedure.

'An operation?'

'Sort of, yeah.'

'And you'll be fine.'

'Of course.'

'Well, that's – that's a relief.'

'Yes,' he agreed, 'although being a Wolffie does mean that I have to be careful. Can't over-exercise.'

'No problem there.' She smiled.

'Or travel,' he said. 'At least, not for a while.'

'Ah. Cambodia.'

'On hold,' Snake told her. He glanced away. 'Anyway, it might be better to wait –'

'Yes –'

'Until we're both ready,' he said.

Thereafter it became an afternoon in which to speak quietly of music and games and stories, and avoid all talk of hearts and sadness. Tillie was grateful for the interlude. Later, as she waited for Susan and the car that would spirit her home, she thought how remarkable it was that Snake had never once judged her or her actions. She could think of no one else, not even her father, to whom she could say, 'This is who I am,' and hear the clear and immediate reply, 'Yes, that is who you are.'

Gilbert folded his fingers, flexed them, unfolded them, cracked one knuckle, another.

'Progress?' he asked.

Less sad but not feeling obviously happy either.

'So you're suspended?'

Eventually she agreed. The process has suspended me. I'm like one of those dragonflies in your picture, sitting on the surface of the water.

Gilbert nodded.

'Ready to rise?'

Not yet, not yet, but I do feel like it's a possibility whereas before –

'Ready to stop sinking?'

More that, yes.

'Suspension,' said Gilbert. 'Tillie Bassett, I too am suspended … somewhere between knowledge and imagination. Between the love I want and the love I have. Between hope and despair. And yes, suspended between sadness and happiness, like all of us –'

'Am I better?'

'You're on the surface,' said Gilbert. 'Isn't that fantastic?'

It was – but last night, again, there'd been the girl who fell from the balcony and flew –

'Now what?' she asked.

'Continue,' he suggested, and Tillie agreed.

PART 3

A crisp, astral night in May when she read:

> Lately I've discovered a powerful wish;
> I'd really like to be a fish.
> Not one that ends up in a dish
> described by diners as delish,
> but a fish with fins and a tail to swish;
> a swimming silvery living fish.
>
> You might ask why this should be;
> what on earth's come over me?
> It's really simple; I want to swim free,
> to at I please and be happy.
> Perhaps I might even meet Tillie B;
> two fish together in the calm blue sea.

This time, she did reply.

Tillie (keeping it light): *Hi Jed. That's funny and clever so thank you for sharing. You're a talented poet but I am too busy being a person to EVER become a fish. Good luck with your dreams!*

Jed: *At last, she speaks! Hallo-ciao-bonjour-gday, how are you?*

Tillie: *Okay thanks. Not being rude here but this kind of thing is not for me, sorry.*

Jed: *Kind of thing? Like chatting? Hey Tillie Bee of Brisbane Citee, no probs but no harm intended either. Enjoyed meeting you way back whenever it was, would like to meet again.*

Tillie: *Don't think that's possible or good idea.*

Jed: *One, anything's possible. Two, how can you know if an idea is good unless you try it?* (Picture of fish face with downturned mouth)

Tillie (several minutes later): *I have a boyfriend.*

Jed (immediately): *I have dimples.*

Jed (shortly afterwards): *I am a dimple-fish.*

Jed (several minutes later): *Hey, glad you liked my popo (that's Fish Language for poem). Send you another?*

I have a boyfriend?

She lay in bed, wondering what strange force had produced that particular lie. She, who genuinely tried hard to never lie … he'd known, of course he'd known. *I have dimples. I am a dimple-fish.* Dumb, trite and silly, because her claim was dumb, trite and silly. Jed had answered like with like.

You, who's never had a boyfriend!

Never even had the offer of a boyfriend, which was hardly surprising. Simple matters; some girls were made, as in physically, socially and emotionally constructed, for boyfriends. Some weren't. Lucy Sandello always had a boyfriend, always older with a name like Tyrone or Benjie, with a smoky car, a tattoo on half his arm and money enough to buy Lucy jewellery that she kept locked in a special drawer. Gabby Jenkins had had the same boyfriend since Year Eight, a guy from State High called Esko. Gabby's narrative had never varied; she and Esko were marrying, then travelling, then living in a pole house next to a beach, then having three children. 'We've always wanted three,' she said.

Bronwyn Power insisted that Esko didn't even exist. 'A figure of her imagination,' said Bronwyn sniffily.

'Figment.'

'What I said, Miss Picky.'

Not that it mattered. Tillie knew that even if Esko didn't exist, the point was that he would one day. Esko or a substitute, meaning that Gabby would do exactly as she desired: marry, travel, live next to a beach and have three children. Lovely wife with a lov-er-ly life.

There were always boys on Macy's periphery too, hopeful bug-eyed boys whom she delighted in deflating.

'William Chong is nice.'

'William Chong is a barnacle. He needs to be scraped and discarded.'

'He likes you!'

'Tillie, you really are naïve. William Chong likes the idea of me. The conquest is what matters. William Braindead Chong wants to be the first to proudly proclaim, the American is mine!'

Melodramatic, Tillie had thought, although she hadn't said so. Macy was difficult to dispute.

Sighing, she sat up, found her water glass and drank deeply. Boyfriends ... truth was, she was scared of knowing someone that closely. Not Jed's fault; it was her uncertainty. Her unwillingness to dig too deeply in case she detected things that frightened her.

Why not be online friends? Never been much good at that either, she thought, which meant, by association, never going to be fully accepted or integrated. Online was everything. But there were rules: what you said, how you said it, when and how you posted, memes, symbols and emoticons ... Unlike nearly everyone else that she knew, Tillie found the whole business to be much harder than conversation. Ironic, she thought, that online chat had been invented to replace face-to-face, yet it had evolved into something far more coded and complex than any conversation could ever be. Those rules, most of which were deliberately left unstated so they could be altered at a whim, were bewildering.

Why not be online friends? Because, thought Tillie, I'd mess it up by saying something wrong or just plain idiotic.

Like, *I have a boyfriend.*

Macy in the shadows meant more time to catch up on missed schoolwork, more time to do pretend-research for her father, and play the latest version of 'Philanthropy' ... more time for her quest. When Tillie asked her mother to describe a time when she'd been really happy, Susan ummed for an uncharacteristically long time before suggesting that the question was too difficult, there were so many options from which to choose.

'When you have children –'

'Sorry,' said Tillie, 'I meant you, alone. Without us.'

Because she wanted the individual's take. Susan chewed her lip, reconsidered.

'I was nineteen,' she said.

Susan didn't realise until later, but that had been a happy time because she had travelled. Alone, into Asia and Europe, Africa. The Middle East! Mad, of course, wouldn't do it these days, but back then … nineteen, a mind erupting with possibilities and an inner voice that spoke loudly and insistently of the need to go when and where she wanted.

'Selfish,' she said, 'but freedom is like that. Only selfish people can be properly free because you have to let go of your responsibilities to other people. If that makes sense?'

Tillie nodded.

'Were there other people?' she asked.

'I was an *only* child,' said Susan, 'who at the age of nineteen was heartily sick of being the *only* thing that my parents had in common. So I packed my passport and went.' She sipped at her coffee. 'Tillie, I had no plan. My only real goal was to discover beautiful things.'

Some people, she said, travel to meet other people. Some want to be away from home, or be reminded of how good home is by seeing other places. Some want to go away to a place that's like home – 'Most Americans,' she said, 'seem to think that the world should be full of mini-Americas.' Some want challenge or discomfort, others parade as travellers because to do so is exotic and life-giving, some seek to escape … 'I travelled for beauty,' said Susan. 'Found it too, in all sorts of places. To answer your question, I think that was what made me happiest – discovering that beauty existed everywhere. Once I knew how to look.'

How was that? Perhaps beauty remained quietly within its own space, sustained by its own beating heart as it waited for the arrival of the true searchers?

'Tell you a story,' said Susan, 'to illustrate my point. I was in northern Spain, a city called Bilbao, and there was a young man sitting on the side of the street with a sack, his blanket and his dog. He was whittling. Carving. He had a couple of short blades, some softwood and a pot of glue, and he was making a ship. It was a single-masted ship, like a cutter. He had one on display and it was amazing. Perfect and delicate … beautiful. Of course, I was entranced by this, so I stood back and watched him work. Sometimes people stopped and gave him a coin or said something nice about his ships, but mostly they just hurried on by because that's what people do. We're all too busy, too self-absorbed to look at a beggar's ship.'

'Did you buy the ship?' asked Tillie.

'No,' said her mother. 'I could've done, I suppose, but for me it was the process … Anyway, he was nearly finished when the police came. Three of them, big men. They spoke with him briefly, then, for no reason that I could see or hear, one of them lifted his boot and stomped on the ship that he was making. Not the display model, the one that he held in his hands. Smashed it to a pulp.'

The one that he held in his hands …

'Tillie, I was devastated. I was also ashamed that I was watching this from the other side of the street and doing nothing to assist, but I didn't really have a choice. Not there, in that city, that country, as a guest … Eventually they moved him on. Made him gather his sack and his blanket, his dog, the leftover pieces of the ship, and leave. He was in front of a bank and a fashion shop – I don't know. It was senseless.'

Tillie could see the young man's face, stretched by tiredness and fear –

'But this,' said Susan, quietly triumphant, 'this. He walked away and so did the police, in a different direction. They were swaggering, laughing; I hated them so much! Then a lovely thing … A shop owner came out, called out to the beggar and offered a space in front of his shop, on a different corner. So the man resettled and got some more wood out of his sack and started again – and I thought, that's it. That's the key. They might stomp on his work and move him on, they might even do worse, but nothing, nothing will take away the urge that he has –'

To whittle his ships

'To make something beautiful,' said Susan. 'And thereby survive.'

They organised home-made pizza for dinner, Susan suggesting that Tillie cut the pineapple, bacon, mushrooms, squeeze a garlic clove, maybe even assemble the ingredients … Time you learned to cook more than toast or stuff from the freezer.

Henry was dining with friends in the city before going on to a meeting – the Cloud Appreciation Society, she wondered? – so it was just Tillie and her mother, Susan unusually relaxed as she announced that her design for the commission had finally been approved, all systems go.

'Great, Mum. Well done.'

'Thanks!' Susan waited for a moment then said, 'Haven't seen anything of Macy for a while. Problem?'

We're polite, thought Tillie. We nod, we say hello. Sit within the shield of the Group.

'Difference of opinion,' she said.

'Happens,' Susan told her briskly. 'Boring old world if everyone agreed all the time. One prerequisite for my friends: don't automatically accept what I say. Challenge, and we'll get on fine.'

The pizza, which smelled delicious, steamed between them.

Susan said, 'Sweetie, if it's meant to be, then …' She paused before asking, 'By the way, what's going on with Rosie?'

Dear Tillie,
My best and dearest collection …

I see you in a swaddling shawl. The shawl was a gift from your aunt Carole. It had a tiny book embroidered in one corner and an angel in another. How apt! We still have it, wrapped in plastic, in a box beneath the stairs.

Inside the shawl you glow like a gem. Not long after you were born I remember thinking, as a child in Pembrooke I always wanted a moonstone for my collection. And now I have one.

I see you holding Oompa, the 'ephelant' that went everywhere with us. Oompa was dragged and thrown and slobbered on, but he always came back for more. Until the day that he stayed in the corner with the other animals and we didn't know why.

'What's wrong with Oompa?'

'He's sick. He has to stay in bed.'

Tillie, something I've never told you: we kept Oompa. He's also in that box beneath the stairs. No doubt he needs a good clean and a few stitches in his trunk – but I'll bet he still loves you.

I see your pale golden curls. When you were about four, Susan told you that all the wedding rings that had ever been lost in the world had gathered on your head. She said, when people love each other properly the wedding rings will return to their fingers. Amazingly, from that point on your hair did grow darker and straighter. It's still wonderful hair and very much you but, we are parents; we will always remember the wedding rings.

I see you sleeping at the end of a summer day beneath the old fig tree at Welch Street. You lay on the grass with your thumb in your mouth and a butterfly landed on your cheek. It was a monarch, with amber drips and spots of white. Rather than watch the butterfly, I should've picked you up and put you into bed, but I didn't want to because that would've been like disturbing a dream.

I see you racing around the sprinkler in the backyard. 'Daddy, don't turn on the water, please don't, don't – eeek! You did!'

Yes, I did. Every time. Like we both wanted.

I see Rosie teaching you the rules for handball. Remember those endless games on the driveway? In, out, double, interference ... When I suggested that we write out the rules, Rosie said no because 'then I won't be able to make them up.'

I see you in uniform and remember thinking that somehow you had become older and were now going to be cared for by other people. How strange it seemed, that our little Tillie would be in a place where we wouldn't be. Rosie couldn't wait to go to school, but you were always more reluctant.

I see you walking around the front garden re-christening the flowers and plants. You wanted to give them the names of your new school friends – Annabel, Amanda, Shelby, Laura. I remember saying, 'Hey, Tillie, that's a rose,' and your immediate reply was, 'Not to me.' I'm pretty sure that rose became Judy Pasadena, from three doors down.

I see your face when I said no and, for the first time, you thought about disagreeing with me. It was a primary school sleepover. Justine's place? Jane's? Anyway, she was a decent girl from a decent family – but I was being irrational. I didn't want to let you go because I was scared of losing you, not just for that night but for always. Susan changed my mind by reminding me how important it was for you to have friendships. I dropped you off, drove home and found your mother in her studio, crying.

I see the hurt in you when Rodger the Lodger went wandering and never came back and you knew – we all knew – that he was too old and had gone somewhere quiet and dark to die. I hated being unable to stop your grief but I knew that it was right that I could not do so. Some things must be negotiated by the self. No one can teach you how to grieve, just as no one can teach you how to love.

I see you growing and finding your voice and learning rights from wrongs and distinguishing those who are worth persisting with from those who are less so and clarifying your ideas and wanting justice, and I know that this is my best and dearest collection, the memories and thoughts and images that sustain me.

Tillie, I am wistful as you grow away from us – and you must! – but I am also thrilled and extremely grateful for who you have become. Rosie too, of course. Over time I have learned to cherish the differences in my daughters – and the samenesses, because you and Rosie are more alike than you could ever believe. Integrity, insight. An inclination to care. You two are both call and echo.

Now, who else is in my collection? Who else stands in the background, by my side, at the forefront? Who helps to create and recreate the light?

Your mother, of course.

Tillie, when you spend year after year with one person, growing further and further into your love, it is like a slow dance, a waltz perhaps, but with heightened moments. In dancing terms those moments might be a lift or a twirl or a jump or a slide, all exhilarating – but it is the rest of the dance, the gentler, more repetitive rhythms and movements, that is of most importance.

Susan made me happy when I first met her because she was everything that I was not. She was bold, creative, adventurous, outspoken – a fitted opposite. I loved the fact that she was so staunchly herself and unlike me. One of me, I felt certain, was more than enough weight for any world to bear.

Simply put, I had to marry her.

While I will not deny that there have been some challenges in our lives together, over time we have both come to know that each of us cannot be truly happy without first deciding to make the other happy. It is a shared mission, for the best of happiness is achieved when we serve ourselves by serving others. Helping each other to overcome our fears and realise our desires, making each other smile and feel that we are always wanted, that our place is always by each other's side; these things remain, for me, the kinds of joy that I want in my life. Her happiness becomes my happiness and mine, hers. In helping each other, and hopefully *helping our children, we can be content.*

So, in this way, we will pledge to maintain and add to our best and dearest collection; all that we have been and are, together.

That's all for now,

With much love, Dad

The web page loaded quickly.

Parkhill Private School, District of Philadelphia. As God Is Our Witness.

She roamed the banner – *Admissions, Curriculum, Alumni* – before clicking on *Campus Life* and seeing images of smiling students in the library or playing volleyball, students running happily around an athletics track or conducting science experiments in a joyous kind of way.

The name had finally come to her and now, looking at the images, she was certain that it was the right school. Once, Macy had mentioned their 'dumb' uniforms. 'Chocolate with a gold trim,' she'd said. 'We looked like Easter eggs.'

So, right uniforms, right school. Tillie flicked through hyperlinks but no school would mention such a traumatic event on their website. New search required. She tapped a phrase into Google and waited.

No hits. The phrase splintered into other areas, including a return to Parkhill's web page. Perhaps the wording was wrong? She reorganised the phrase and pressed Enter.

Same results.

Non-results.

Okay, broaden. She deleted the phrase and typed another, more generic: *US school shootings last five years.* The names tumbled horribly forth: Harrisburg, Jacksonville, California, Miami, Marysville, Oregon, Salisbury, Des Moines … Philadelphia.

Clicked the link. Two killed and five wounded at a university. Tillie didn't read the entry, instead typing a new search, *US high school shootings last five years Philadelphia.*

Lists, maps, articles, explanations. Calls for tighter gun laws, counter-claims as to why these wouldn't work. But nothing from Philadelphia, nothing from Parkhill Private.

She said, 'I heard from Jed.'

Macy sat across the lunch table. She was eating cubes of apple and melon from a plastic tub.

'Who?' said Gemma Britten.

Tillie ignored Gemma – always good practice – and waited.

Macy said, 'I didn't think –' then stopped, ate some more, the juice enlivening her lips.

'He wrote a poem,' Tillie said. 'It was okay. Funny.'

'Who?' said Gemma again.

'That's nice.' Macy placed the lid on the tub, pushed it down and stood. 'Gotta go, gang. Catch ya later.'

Tillie said quickly, 'Come over this afternoon. I really need to talk to you.'

Not Jed … Philadelphia.

'Kinda busy.' Macy pulled her hair back, tubed it and flicked on a band.

'Please, Macy. It's important.'

'Uh-huh.' There was such distance in Macy's voice that Tillie could only think of the desert that her father had described in his first instalment, that cold lonely place where stillness reigned – until the wind rose without warning, turned grit into a weapon.

She tried to keep her face expressionless.

Macy said, 'Well, maybe. Sometime. But not this afternoon.'

She strode away.

The bell rang, a hungry magpie landed on the edge of their table and Gemma Britten said, 'Tillie, you can talk to me if you want. Is Jed your boyfriend?'

May in Brisbane is cooler, with a kinder sun. The tree cycle of flowering and shedding slows to a squeeze. The breeze is a scent that flutters through the river channel and drapes the hills and suburbs like muslin. Even the traffic unwinds; there are less snarls as people sigh, smile vaguely and wander towards their homes, families and twilit gardens, there to sit, be tired, rejoice.

Snake had been told he should walk home from school, a mild form of exercise, so Tillie walked with him along avenues overshadowed by unruly poinsettias and apartment blocks. Small talk or silence for several streets until –

'I know she's your friend,' said Snake.

Is? Was? Tillie wasn't sure any more.

'Doesn't mean that you have to be quite so ... dependent.'

'Am I?'

'Seems that way,' he said carefully. 'As in, always checking in.'

A thought, an idea, an opinion. World view.

'Don't get angry,' he said.

'I'm not.'

'I just think, ever since she arrived and sort of chose you –'

Why was that, Tillie wondered. Why nothing-me? Snake would never say, but she sensed the answer, had sensed it for some time now; because you're one of those people who cleaves themselves to another's personality and style rather than asserting your own … one of those people who is not just afraid of the universal black dust but afraid of being you.

Tillie's adaptable!

Tillie's pliable.

Tillie's a great friend!

Tillie belongs to other people.

She said, 'I know, but sometimes it feels like –'

'What?'

A whisper. 'Without her, I'm lost. Can't cope –'

'You can.'

But so, so difficult to forgo that strength, be on your own –

'Look,' said Snake. He stopped walking and pointed to the base of a tree. A sinewy trunk twisted and arose before evolving into branches that covered a roof, crept like witches' fingers into gutters and hovered dangerously close to the overhead wires.

'Where?'

'Between the roots,' he said. 'See how it is. Down there, nothing grows. There's no light, and any nutrients that might exist are sucked up by the tree for its own purposes.'

Tillie got the analogy. Remembered that biology unit from last year … *Epiphytes use other plants for support without actually affecting the host.*

'I think you're being a bit harsh,' she said.

'Maybe.' Snake blinked, slid his hands into his pockets. 'Maybe I have to be.'

They walked to the end of the street, cut through an easement.

'I'm just saying, you don't need her approval. You can, you know, go your own way.'

A bloke snipping his hedge, a motorbike thundering by. They drifted further, stopped outside Snake's house. In the front yard Lizzie was being pushed in a tyre swing by Petey.

Snake grimaced. 'Wait for the explosion,' he said, dropping his bag off his shoulder. She expected him to go through the front gate but he loitered, scraping at the path with his shoe.

'Next weekend,' he said, 'that dance.'

Senior disco … first opportunity for the Year Tens to join the Big School. As in, spend three hours in a dark corner with the other uncomfortables, drink warm cola and go home with a sick stomach and throbbing ears.

'Would you like to go?' Snake asked.

You. Me. Disco?

Tillie said, 'You never go to things like that.'

Snake looked embarrassed. 'First time for everything,' he said. 'Hey, I just want to do something normal.'

You and me? At a disco?

'Stop being so serious, you know. I'm always serious.'

Like it was an illness. Or a syndrome.

'Snake,' she asked, 'is this a date?'

He reddened and nearly smiled, opened the gate, swung his bag back and forth as if on a pivot. 'If you like,' he said before going to the tyre swing to placate, reorganise.

Tillie, whose appetite had returned of late, ate a square of fruit cake before following a rackety noise into her mother's studio. Susan was clad in earmuffs and a mask. She was wrestling with a large sheet of timber ply and a jigsaw, and eventually sliced a long arc into the outer third of the ply. The severed piece clattered to the floor. Susan retrieved it, stood up and saw Tillie. She switched off the tool, placed it carefully on a bench and removed her mask and earmuffs.

'Well,' she said, 'I'm either going to need soundproofing or a place that's so remote, no one can hear. Can't imagine the neighbours will be too thrilled if I keep going like this. How was school?'

Tillie murmured an okayness, sat on a stool. She said, 'Mum, I think I've been trying so hard to be like other people –'

Susan's eyes flickered.

'Go on,' she said.

'That I've forgotten how to be me,' said Tillie … Yes, she thought, yes, too much time worrying about why she wasn't like this person, or how she could modify herself to be like that person. Too much agony spent on the notion that those who were loved by all and sundry didn't have blobby knees or strange fears or get themselves ludicrously upset about dreams and mirrors, grey hairs, disappearing geckos –

Susan said, 'Tillie, we all make adjustments. We go to Sydney, I'm a different person with your grandparents than I am normally. Agreed?'

Grinding, snapping … those trips, although infrequent, did alter her mother.

'Different again with people from the industry,' said Susan. 'Eduardo thinks I'm a complete softie.'

Eduardo, president of a private organisation that supplied funding to artists, had been around for dinner a couple of times. Cooked by Henry.

'My point being, everyone adjusts – but it should never be to the extent that you lose the real you. Present an alternative *side* by all means, but don't present an alternative *person*.'

As in, with Macy?

Further thought required. Tillie left the stool, wandered around her mother's workbench. At one end there was a drawing done on a large sheet of graph paper. Tillie saw curves and circular holes, three identical shapes intertwined to form a dramatic whole that was as much art as it was object.

'What's this?' she asked.

'Demanding.' Susan pushed back an unruly fistful of hair. 'But for all that, I am happy with the design. I was inspired by certain things.'

She came forward, faced Tillie and touched her hand.

'Rosie's pregnant, isn't she?'

A moment … Tillie nodded.

'Doesn't want to tell me?'

'Mum, she can't.'

Susan's eyes betrayed her. 'I understand that,' she said sadly.

In Psych today we did this session on memory and it was actually a bit interesting which makes a change for Psych (and school). I always thought that your memory was like this library full of books (what else would a library be full of, haha). That book over there describes when I fell out of the fig tree and sprained my wrist, whereas that book is the moment SHE came back from wherever and I thought oh no this can't be happening everything was going SO WELL. That book is riding my bike to the shop alone when I was eight and seeing that man in the park (foul!) and that book is when Dad brought home Rodger the pathetic old darling.

So memory (I thought) is a massive bunch of books and every day you're adding more books which means the library keeps getting bigger and bigger, even though there are books that fall off the shelf and go — where? Onto the floor? If they're on the floor, they can always be picked up again. So do they go someplace else like into a deep hole which is actually an incinarator so they are burned forever more? Or maybe they go to the Planet of Lost Memories which would be a pretty interesting place to visit though scary because if a memory is good then you're going to try hard not to lose it, right? So the PLM must have a whole bunch of scary/bad memories rattling around like skeletons in the closet.

Anyway turns out I was wrong (a bit). Memory isn't a library but LOTS of libraries with connecting corridors and overpasses and tunnels. Like a giant network of libraries. So that book does describe me falling out of the fig tree but there's a different book in a different library that has my thoughts as I fell and a different book again that has me in hospital and reminds me how that felt and how I just wanted Dad in the room. The whole incident isn't just in one book, there are lots, and if I want to remember Fig Tree Fall properly I have to get all the books together, put them in order then re-read them which is what the old brain does, pretty amazing.

Thinking about that since I got home I've worked out the problem with Birthday Party memory. I've only got bits because I haven't been to all the libraries haven't pulled all the books. I've got the cake book and the presents book Then I've got The walking up book and the bandaged-head book and the look-at-my-horrible-face book and the Mum-endlessly-sobbing book and all those sorries and everything afterwards (a library on its own) but I haven't got the in-between book. Which is the one I need to find. I've seen it and read the blurb so I know there are three chapters: Chapter What Happened which I know most of but not all, Chapter How It Happened which I've only read some of and Chapter Why It Happened which I have either forgotten or never read. Meaning Birthday Party memory is incomplete and even though it's OBVIOUSLY BAD and a definite candidate for the Planet of Lost Memories I still need to know.

So —

Gunna ask Dad sometime soon. Gunna say, Henry old mate, there's a book missing. Find it for me?

And if that doesn't work I'll put on my suit of armour grab my sword and ask her.

On Wednesday in drama they were due to pair up and perform improvs based on place and emotion: Restaurant–Greed, Shop–Envy. Ms Andrewartha drew names from her magical silver box, Tillie first followed by Simone Varela.

'Simone? Where are you?'

'Gone,' said Brad Mitchelton.

'Gone where?'

'Left school, Miss.' A girl, Holly, grinned wickedly and motioned a large stomach. 'Had to.'

The class laughed, Ms Andrewartha looked befuddled and Tillie was assigned a new partner, Geraldine, who didn't speak so was doing drama to lift her self-confidence.

At morning recess she went to where Simone would normally have sat but Helena Godwin was there alone. Helena was an awkward florid girl, largely unnoticed outside of being Simone's friend.

'She's not pregnant!' said Helena indignantly. 'Holly and those girls, they're idiots. They spread lies then sit back and watch the fallout … I hate them.'

Tillie could see tears in the other girl's eyes. She said, 'They're jealous, I guess.'

'I know. Jealous idiots.'

A group passed by. One girl pointed but quickened her walk when Helena glared.

Tillie said, 'Where is Simone?'

'Don't know.' Helena flushed, stared at the trees. 'Home. Another school. Timbuktu.'

'You haven't spoken –'

'Not since she left, no. Which was last Friday. I tried all weekend but she wouldn't answer her phone, then I got some message about the number no longer being in service. She wasn't online and she wouldn't answer the door at home. When her mother did, I asked if I could see Simone and she told me to go away. She said, Simone wants nothing to do with her old school or any of the people there. Thankfully, she said. Thankfully!'

Tillie didn't know how to respond.

Helena muttered, 'She was my best friend. Doesn't that count for something?'

Should.

'Not always,' Tillie suggested gently.

'People don't realise,' said Helena, 'what Simone went through, and they don't realise how much I helped her. Tillie, you won't say anything?'

'No.'

'I trust you, okay? Simone trusted you too, she said so. Thing is, after that stupid musical she went all weird, started saying and doing weird stuff. Like, first of all she was banging on about Jesus and how it was a crock, and I thought, okay, the show's got to her but, you know, it'll pass. But it got worse – what's the point, no Jesus means no purpose, blah-blah-blah – and I'm trying to talk her through it every day, which was when I saw what she was really doing.'

Tillie waited.

'Cuts,' said Helena. 'Big cuts. Did you notice how lately she always wore the blazer, even when it was hot? That's why. Last week I saw blood on the cuff and I thought, that's wrong so I pulled up the sleeve before she could stop me and that's when I saw. We had this really long argument and Simone said, so what, do what I like, butt out, which was really unlike her, then on Friday she went home at lunchtime and that was that.'

'Did you tell anyone?'

'Her mum,' sniffed Helena. 'I had to.'

'What did her mum say?'

'She said to stop meddling.' Helena took a tissue from her pocket and wiped her face. 'Then she said, get out of our lives, you're not welcome any more.'

In the gymnasium there were coloured streamers and balloon clusters. A temporary dance floor had been laid in the centre, flanked by enormous speakers. Groups of girls were on the floor, gaudy tops and hairpieces giving them the appearance of jiggling bouquets. Boys with slicked sideburns and skintight tees patrolled the perimeter of the dance floor or mustered near the exits, looking for a chance to slip past the teacher-guards and sneak into their beloved shadows.

Snake brought her a plastic cup of something tepid and orange.

'Thanks.'

They watched the dancers, Tillie suddenly aware of Snake's extended height. When did that happen? There was a new heaviness to him as well … She sneaked a glance. Trick of the strobe or fluff on his jaw?

A new song, *doof-doof* splintering the humid air as a hundred cheered and thronged to the dance floor … Snake's lips moved.

'Can't hear you!'

He gestured to a spot further away and they speed-walked.

'I said, this music –'

Is sucky. Not his style at all and a sacrifice, she thought, to bring her here. A kindness. She smiled, touched his arm, very warm, but Snake seemed to shiver. They reverted to watching the dancers and there, on the edge but forcing her way into the sanctum, was Macy. She was spinning and freestyling opposite –

William Chong. Laugh-or-cry moment, Tillie wasn't sure.

Finally the music subsided, temporarily replaced by the announcement of lucky door prizes.

Snake said, 'Hey, we *can* dance if you like –'

'I don't mind –'

'It's just, I have to take it easy. Dance like a dork, you know –'

'My usual style,' said Tillie, and Snake smiled.

'So,' he said, 'I had my follow-up tests yesterday. The doctors think it might be better, long term, if I have that operation.'

She looked at his pale freckly face, ginger dreads framing and coiling.

'It's all done with radio frequency,' he explained. 'They take away the extra cable, no more electrical overload.'

'When?' she asked.

'Don't know. Soon.'

The music started again, the breath and ache of a popular ballad.

'Come on,' said Tillie. 'This one we can do.'

Not so much a dance as a shuffle, Tillie now fully aware of Snake's height and heaviness, the gentlemanly placement of his hands. Later, maybe out of sight, maybe not; the mix of mint and orange in his trembling mouth.

Dear Tillie,

This will be my final reflection on your very important question.

As I've already indicated, my father was a difficult man. You have known very little about him, not just because he died before you were born but also because I have chosen to hide his character from you and Rosie. Enough trials occur in the course of normal living and I saw little purpose in adding another. That may have been a mistake but it was a choice that I made a long time ago so I must live with it.

That said, as I have grown older I have become more forgiving of the burdens of my childhood. I can still feel the heat of my father's terrible anger but now believe that he was suffering from an illness that, typical of his generation, he refused to have diagnosed and treated. His abuse of myself, my sisters and our mother, while awful and unfair, was clearly the consequence of a mental problem that he could never properly control or resolve.

I'm guessing that he hated himself more than he ever hated us.

Tillie, my father was swamped by the darkness of his own unhappiness. As a younger man he used sport as a way of dealing with this. Being with mates, starring in a match, having a win, feeling the applause of the crowd – these moments gave him temporary relief from the horror of how he really felt. Given that, what a disappointment it must have been for him to wreck not one but both knees and be told by surgeons that he would never again play sport. What further disappointment to realise that his son, through whom he might hope to live a reproduction of his old life, did not share his sporting talent or desire, and that his daughters more closely resembled his wife, the woman whom he was certain could no longer value or love him.

Sport became the bitter past. He couldn't watch it without being devastated that he wasn't playing. He didn't want to coach a team or work around the club because of all the reminders – the honours boards and photos and blokes patting him on the back and saying bad luck, Basso, you were the best. Were.

So he turned from it all and lost himself in a haze of anger. The unhappiness that he had mostly managed to avoid now flooded into him and we, his children, felt the brunt of his disillusionment. Great pain for us but terrible for him too, a prison wall.

Tillie, as much as we might like to think otherwise, we are all created as a blend – of those things unique to us, those given to us by our situations and those inherited from our makers. The point being, we all inherit something. Your mother sees the world as organic and connected; so do you. Rosie has Susan's independent spirit and fire; you have my natural reticence.

I too inherited. I have my mother's shyness and passivity – and I have my father's darkness. Once I had worked this out, I decided that I did not have his anger, so my response to the darkness would be different. I would withdraw from the world, but with purpose. Hence my collections; not just protection from him but protection from myself. Hence also my desire that each collection be perfect and complete. Tillie, I have cherished all of my collections and in so doing, I have sought the light. My father was never able to do this.

For a long time I thought that I hated him. As a child I used to go out to the wood shed, sit alone with the spiders, and wish that my father would die. As a younger man, making my way in the world, I cut all contact with him. I thought, you are nothing to me. I do not care for you in any way, I do not wish to know you.

Not long after my twenty-third birthday, my mother rang to tell me that he had passed away. Medically, he had a heart attack but my mother believed otherwise, that he could see no reason to keep on living.

Was I happy that this angry, abusive man was finally out of my life?

No! I was distraught because I had lost the chance for redemption. My father and I will never resolve our differences – and it is a terrible thing for someone to leave this earth without having first reconciled the wrongs.

I learned too late: as my parent, he is never out of my life.

I also learned that I must take some blame for this. The child-me was confused and afraid, but the man-me should not have opted to simply accept my father's darkness. I should have returned home, faced my father and said, Dad, this is wrong. We need to sort this out. We need to get back together as a family and find peace with each other.

Tillie, all of this leads me to this belief – that happiness stands alongside truth. If we truly want to be happy then we must be honest in who we are *with others and who we are with ourselves, and we must love with the same generosity that we wish to be loved. The person who wakes each day and goes to sleep each night with only truth in between has achieved the best that any human can hope for. Of all of us, that person is most likely to be happy.*

Love always, Dad

A quiet Sunday morning, her parents still asleep. Drawn to the window by a kookaburra calling for rain, Tillie saw a muddy sky, trees shivering as they waited for the light.

She dressed and went to the bathroom to wash her face and hands. As usual, the gloating mirror awaited. She took a towel from the rack, reached out and –

No.

Don't.

Put the towel back, nice and straight, thinking Dad likes the towels to be straight. She swished cold water into the basin, washed away the night hours, dried herself and turned back to the mirror.

Look, she said to herself, with determination. Look properly.

Look and think: those are the grey eyes that other people have said they liked and wished were their own. There is the nose that my mum (thankfully) gave me. There, on my forehead, is my dad's worry line but thinner, not fully developed. That's my own, unique-to-Tillie skin, and it's a good colour, a glowy colour, and that's my hair, which used to be made of wedding rings, and those are my lips that –

She smiled.

'Should I come over?' he'd asked.

'Please,' she'd agreed.

A quiet Sunday morning. Last night she'd promised to get up early and head to the marketplace, get some milk. 'And eggs,' said Henry, his voice crackling like an old radio show. 'We're out of eggs.'

His routine: two boiled eggs, four minutes, every morning. Funny? No, survival.

She let herself out of the house, being careful not to bang the door. The air was clean and sharp. The shrubs lining the front path had lost their fragrance to winter but there was still pleasure to be had in their closed-off backs and hardened twigs.

Tillie stopped at the gate and looked back. When she was born they'd lived in a house in Welch Street. Rosie had frequently said that 'the old place' was better – less sprawl, more character – but Tillie could only really remember this house, with its long hallway that was good for sock-sliding, and windows that didn't open whenever it rained because the timber had swelled, and the roof leaks that her father thought he'd fixed but hadn't. The kitchen, with small orange and green tiles that were so deliciously retro, said her mother, that they must stay, Susan's studio, formerly a garage, her father's study with what he jokingly referred to as its elaborate view – actually a rusted fence that separated their house from that of Mr and Mrs Prashad (and a fluctuating number of other Prashads) next door.

Just a house, she'd always thought.

But more. A home. *Their* home. Thirteen years of words and looks and thoughts soaked into the walls and ceilings, the furniture, the floorboards. Soaked into each other. Her family's capacity to absorb and continue had been their offering. Jagged, occasionally, but there nevertheless. Always there.

Low-fat milk and XL eggs. As Tillie left the marketplace she saw Mrs Cooper carrying a shopping bag and sweeping the footpath with her cane, a small white ball on the end.

'Mrs Cooper? It's Tillie, Tillie Bassett.'

'Susan's daughter. Hallo, dear.'

'Can I take your bag?'

She did so and they walked together towards Mrs Cooper's street. Tillie said, 'I wanted to tell you how much – how wonderful your paintings are.'

'That's very kind. Susan has said that you are a kind girl.'

Tillie blushed … The thought came to her quickly and beautifully, a bird landing.

'Mrs Cooper,' she said, 'your paintings – they're a bit dusty. I could clean them, if you like. I'd be very careful. I know how precious they must be.'

Quiet now, Tillie forging on.

'Clean them and maybe even bring one or two upstairs. They're so lovely and' – a word, what word? – 'rich.' She gulped then said, 'Sorry, I just think they belong in the light rather than down in there.'

'In the gloom?'

'Yes. Sorry.'

'Oh, don't be,' said Mrs Cooper. 'Nice to hear a young voice. Young ideas.'

They stopped at the front gate. Tillie put the shopping bag into Mrs Cooper's hand. Mrs Cooper said, 'Tillie, you're kind, but – I don't know. I can no longer see my work so –'

'I could describe the paintings to you,' Tillie told her.

Mrs Cooper was silent.

'So you could see them again,' said Tillie quickly. 'It's not the same, I know, but –'

A sprinkle of rain made Mrs Cooper lift her battered face and sniff the air. She allowed the rain to massage the creases on her skin before pushing at the gate and saying, 'Your mother's daughter, that's for sure. Tillie, it's wet out here. Let's go inside.'

He said, 'I'm not very good at this.'

'Me either. Never had a boyfriend before.'

His laugh was throaty.

'What?'

'That word,' he said. '*Boyfriend*. Hard to believe.'

'Sounds okay, though?'

'Yeah,' he said. 'Sounds good. Better than I ever thought.'

He scratched the side of his nose and said, 'Hey?'

'What?'

'I don't want to lose –'

'What?'

'How we were.'

'You've always been my best friend.'

'Have I? That's cool. You've always –'

'We won't lose that.'

'I hope not. Please –'

'We'll just hold hands and be best friends. Like this.'

'Okay. Okay.'

'See? It's easy.'

'Yeah. Pretty much. Um, do other best friends do this kind of thing?'

'Don't know,' said Tillie. 'Don't care. We do.'

Dr Ev welcomed her, sat her down, surveyed her for a moment and said, 'You look well.'

She felt pretty good, that was true. More alive, waking muscles, shifting blood. She remembered their cat, Rodger the Lodger, being sick with cat flu. He hadn't looked too bad on the outside, skinnier maybe, but his eyes had told the tale. They were dull, weepy and mucky. When Rodger recovered, his eyes shone and danced.

'Cat's back,' said Susan, giving Rodger an extra spoonful of tuna.

Tillie stripped down for testing. Weight, better. Blood pressure, fine. Heart, normal. No, she thought with a secret smile, heart bigger. Heart blossoming!

Dr Ev put away her stethoscope, leaned forward and said, 'Sleep?'

'Yes,' Tillie told her. As in, not perfect but I am sleeping. Most nights now the girl stays on the balcony, only looks at the edge. Sometimes she even pulls back.

'Good,' said Dr Ev. 'Exercise?'

'Yes.'

'Cycle?'

'Walking,' said Tillie and they both grinned.

'Tell me about the sadness,' said Dr Ev.

Not gone. Never gone. Part of me, part of –

'I feel more in control,' said Tillie.

'Great! Any particular reason for that?'

Back to causality. Was there a reason? She wasn't sure. Something to do with understanding? With connectedness?

Love?

'Lots of reasons,' she said. The known and not-so.

In the car, her father was reading a magazine about model yachts, taking notes on his iPad.

'Okay?'

Tillie nodded. As always, Henry waited for her to fasten her seat belt before he started the car.

She said, 'Dad, Rosie let me read her diary for my project.'

'Her diary?'

'She wrote a diary when she was about my age.'

'Did she? I never knew.'

One more question, thought Tillie. Going to hurt, I know, but without this –

Happiness stands alongside truth.

She said, 'Rosie wrote about being at a birthday party when something bad happened. She said her memory was incomplete and she was going to find out more. The next entry, she wrote one line – *I will never forgive* – and that was that.

The diary stopped.'

Her father's face, as blank and flat as old concrete.

'What happened?' asked Tillie.

Tuesday after school, a message indicator popped on to her screen. Tillie clicked on it and read:

Hey there, I know you said you don't want this chatting thing and that's cool, your call, BUT – I just wanted you to know that things have changed in my life and I won't be in contact any more. To cut a dumb story short, I got kicked out of home and I'm moving south to live with Dad. Who's not at Byron Bay, like he always said but further south at a place called Iluka. It's a small town near another small town called Yamba. Apparently Dad's got this old shack and a new girlfriend whose name is Sunni (Soo-Nee) and he's working part-time at a bait shop. He said I can stay with them as long as I don't whinge about no internet or interfere with his life because he's happier now than he's ever been. There's a school at another town so I'll have to catch the bus and he says I need to get weekend work because he can't afford to support me but at least I'll have a room.

Sorry to lay this on you but I thought you should know.

See you in the sea, Jed

She wrote back immediately: *Hey Jed, so sorry to hear about your troubles. It sounds awful. Is there anything I can do to help? Tillie*

Jed (very quickly): *No but thanks anyway. The whole thing is worse than it should be because it was actually Mum who kicked me out. For some strange reason she decided to agree with Fat*

Phil (stepfather) who thinks I'm <u>deliberately undermining</u> their relationship. I got pretty angry at that accusation and said 'no, you're wrong mate' because I don't give a stuff about your stupid relationship, what I care about is that you hurt my mum because you're a coward and a bully and a thug. I thought he'd get stuck into me then and I wish he had because I was ready to belt his oversized pig-head into a distant universe (tough guy, hey?) but instead it was Mum. Don't speak to Phillip like that, after all he's done, where do you think this lovely apartment came from, not your father that's for sure, who do you think pays the bills, your school fees – on and on. So I thought, okay, it's a bunch of garbage but if I apologise then it's over and we can go back to being the family we were before, pathetic but better than nothing – but Mum said, I've had enough of this attitude, pack your bags, you're out of here. I thought she was bluffing but they must have already discussed it because FP said it's the best solution Jed, your father has agreed to take you.

Jed (again): *Leaving this afternoon. Train, bus, bus, ferry.*

Tillie: *Let me know when you arrive and STAY IN TOUCH!*

Jed: *If I can. See what happens.*

Jed (again): *Hey Tillie, I really liked you. When I sent that stuff to you, it was because I liked you. No other reason. I wasn't being stupid. I know it was only one afternoon and evening together but maybe that's all it takes. Just thought you should know.*

Tillie: *I'm sorry. Truly.*

Tillie (again): *Hey, I just looked up Iluka on Wikipedia. Looks like there are lots of places for fish to swim and be free?*

She waited but Jed did not reply. Getting ready to catch the train, she thought, rubbing hard at her eyes. Heading south, wondering.

Suspended, Gilbert would say. Like all of us.

They lived in an apartment on the eighth floor.

'Not the penthouse,' she'd said. 'No views. We look into other apartments. Cranky people live there. Every time they see us, they close the curtains.'

Tillie had only been to the apartment once, that time when they'd sampled the drinks cabinet, Macy saying, your place is sooo much better, it's comfy and homey whereas here is cramped, the air con always breaks down, my dad is a messy old dog … It's super-embarrassing, he leaves his undies lying around. Tillie, you don't want to see the colour of those things, they walk of their own accord –

She rang the bell.

'Hallo, this is Macy!'

'It's me. Tillie.'

A pause long enough for her to rescan the foyer: gleaming tiles, reproduction classical statue amid weeping ferns, tinted windows and a receptionist who did not appear to move. Tillie wondered if he was made of plastic.

'It's open.' Macy's voice again, the sizzle evaporated.

Tillie stepped into the elevator. One side was glass. As the capsule rose, she was able to see the city: tall glassy buildings, pieces of green that had drifted like paper into the shadows cast by those buildings, the river in parts, as if it had been sliced up and redistributed.

A bell dinged, the doors parted. Steeling herself, Tillie

walked along a short corridor. Apartment 82 was indeed open and Macy was inside, sprawled along a divan with a bowl of Cheezels. She was watching a movie on a flat-screen that ate up most of one wall.

Tillie stood awkwardly. Macy picked up the remote, paused the movie and said, 'Well, this is a surprise. You wanna sit down? Or not staying so long?'

Tillie chose the only armchair that was not festooned with newspapers and finance magazines. Glancing around she saw washing-up in the sink, coffee cups on the floor, clothes thrown carelessly over the backs of the dining chairs.

Opening line, only one she could think of.

'I heard from Jed.'

Macy's lack of interest was obvious but Tillie told her a brief version of the story anyway. Macy said, 'Too bad,' looked back to the flat-screen.

'There's something else,' said Tillie.

'Of course.' Macy picked up the remote, tossed and caught it easily. 'You wouldn't come here just to tell me that. Hey, before you begin, let me tell *you* something. Might be interesting. Might even be relevant, you know, to whatever it is you want to say.'

A buzzer went off in the kitchen. Macy ignored it. She said, 'We're going back to the States. My dad's contract is over. He thought about extending, but the money's less than what he's worth. Good experience, he said, but he'll make a lot more back in Philly, or maybe LA. So, yeah.' She shrugged as if none of it mattered and said, 'We head off in a month or so.'

'We'll miss you,' said Tillie. She meant it too. Whatever else had happened, Macy had brightened them somehow –

'Thanks,' said Macy. 'A lie, but well meant. So thanks.'

She stood in one fluid movement and said, 'Is that it?' Tillie didn't answer. Macy went to the kitchen, fiddled with the oven, came back into the main room and said, 'Hey, Tillie, my lie was well meant too. Is that why you're here?'

She nodded. When Macy asked how she'd known, Tillie told her about remembering the name of the school, researching Parkhill, nothing online.

Nothing.

'Well,' said Macy, 'I'd forgotten I told you the name. Hey, whatever. No damage done.'

Tillie said, 'I just want to know why.'

'Really? It isn't obvious?'

'Not to me.'

'Okay. It was – I had to do something. Shake you out of your endless – whatever it was. Lethargy. Misery.'

'But why that?'

'So you could see how selfish it was for you to be behaving that way! Tillie, there are people out there who really are suffering and you –'

'I know that.'

'You're wandering around … Oh, I'm sad, woe is me, poor me, me-me-me. I was trying to make you realise –'

'And to do that, you lied about a school shooting. Of all things … you lied about people being killed and you being under a desk, waiting to die –'

'I had to make it real!'

Tillie, trying to keep an evenness in her voice, asked, 'Macy, was any of it even part way true? That bit about the girl, your friend –'

'Bernie is my cousin's friend. I have met her and she did lose a leg … happened at a different school, in Texas, and it was an accident but –'

'All this,' said Tillie, 'to shake me up. Anything else? Your pop?'

'Hey, he *was* at Vietnam and he *doesn't* talk about it. Look,' she said, 'I'm sorry about the lie –'

'You were so convincing!'

'I've read stuff, seen stuff, we all have. Tillie, believe me, I did what I did with the best of intentions. I just wanted –'

'To shake me up. I get it. So why couldn't you tell me a real story rather than – that?'

'I don't have any real stories,' Macy told her. The idea seemed to surprise her. 'Not of that kind, anyway.'

'Your mum?' suggested Tillie. 'You never mention her.'

'Nothing to mention. I was glad when they divorced; together, they were crap. Look, I've said I'm sorry. And since we're being totally honest here, it wasn't just to shake you up –'

'Then what?' cried Tillie. 'What did you really want?'

'My friend back.' Macy wrapped her arms around her own body, as if to protect it. 'Like we were, first few months.'

Like we were? No, thought Tillie, like you wanted us to be. Exotic-you dragging nothing-me in your sparkling wake because I was exactly the kind of friend you planned for –

someone who would help to raise the pedestal, place you on top and admire without question. Someone who would contribute to you, rather than to themselves.

Macy said, 'It was great back then. You were great. Then – I don't know. You slid.'

Tillie stood. She said, very formally, 'I hope it all goes well for you.'

Macy didn't reply. Tillie was near the doorway when she remembered.

'Did you really have your own quest?' she asked.

'Yes, I did,' said Macy. 'Your dithering-about made me kind of curious so I started to look at, you know, the happiness question for myself. Look beyond the dog and the recipes and the boyfriend. Then I discovered something that interested me, made me want to find out more.'

'Discovered what?' she asked.

'A bunch of Buddhists,' said Macy. Her smile was wry. 'Good people, not so crazy. I even went to some lessons, like an orientation thing. Maybe I'll pursue it in the States, maybe not. Don't know.'

Tillie tried her own smile. It didn't work.

Macy stretched. She said, 'Hey, Matilda Jane, saw you snug as a bug with old Snakey-boy the other day. That's cool. Guess I deserve some credit for that, huh?'

Back along the corridor. The elevator was still there, waiting. Throughout the slow drop Tillie's view of the city was unchanged. As she exited on the ground floor she saw that the foyer still gleamed but the plastic receptionist had departed.

Gilbert ushered her in. He said, 'It's good to see you again.'

Tillie thanked him and they spoke briefly. The quest? Going well, finding out lots, developing some ideas. To share? Not yet. Fine, he said, no problem at all. Now, anything else?

One thing. She plunged, told him about her recurring dream, the girl falling from the balcony. Gilbert sucked briefly on his bottom lip. He said, 'Do you recognise this girl?'

'I don't really see her,' said Tillie. 'Not like that. I mean, she's not faceless but her face isn't – it doesn't seem to be important.'

Gilbert nodded. 'And recently,' he said, 'she's been stepping away from the edge?'

'Yes.'

'How do you feel about that?'

'Better.'

'Whereas before?'

'It was horrible. I knew what was coming but I couldn't stop her. She'd jump off the edge and fall, then when she was close to the ground she'd stop falling and fly, then she'd reach a point somewhere up high –'

'Same point?'

'Don't know. It was just – there. She'd fall again, fly, fall, over and over. I never knew whether I was awake or half-asleep, dreaming or actually seeing her.'

'But now she steps away from the edge. That's good, Tillie.'

'I guess so.'

'Be even better,' said Gilbert, 'if she went inside. Can you make her do that?'

'Maybe. It's not a game … I don't feel like I can just control her –'

'Well, we might try. Close your eyes for a moment and think about the dream.'

'Really?'

'Really.'

'I don't –'

'Just try. Can you see her?'

'It's weird. Normally I'm in bed –'

'Try.'

Opaqueness … a black dot … more black dots, joining, forming … the building, the rush, the knowledge –

'She's there.'

That was a voice. Whose voice? My voice?

'Where is she?'

'She's on the edge. She's about to –'

'Step her back, Tillie, step her back.'

Was it the wind? Did a hand tug at her shoulder? Did a god gently shift –

'She's back.'

'Okay. Now, look behind her. Is there a door?'

'I can't see.'

'Keep looking. A door.'

'There is! I never noticed that –'

'Can she open the door? Does it push or slide?'

'It slides.'

'Uh-huh. Slide it now. Tell me what's inside.'

'Um, a floor and – a lamp. Bright lamp.'

'She can walk through the door, towards the lamp.'

'I suppose. Yes, she –'

'Okay, so she's inside? Inside is good. Bet she feels a whole lot safer.'

'Yes.'

'But tired. All that energy expended on the balcony has left her tired. Might have to go to bed.'

'Okay.'

'Bedroom's out the back, I think.'

'Down the hallway.'

'That's right. Long way back but the lamp is on, the lamp will show the way.'

'There's another door.'

'That's okay. She can open doors, remember? Close them too.'

'Okay.'

'Is she inside the bedroom yet?'

'Ye-e-es.'

'So now she's going to close the door –'

'Mmm –'

'And lie down on the bed. It's warm and comfortable and solid, really solid.'

'She's there.'

'How does it feel?'

'Good. It feels good.'

'I'll bet. Feels good and real and safe. She's closing her eyes –'

'Yes, she is.'

'And rolling onto her side –'

'Yes –'

'And sleeping. Tillie, look. She's asleep. The girl is finally asleep.'

They were all there because Henry had insisted, really insisted, and for once Susan had agreed but softly, a given-up version of Susan, as pliable as her own modelling clay. As the farmhouse had risen from a backdrop of deep olive, Tillie had seen her mother coiling as if afraid; she'd wondered momentarily if Susan would even be able to leave the car.

But Niko had met them with bear hugs and handshakes, his energy propelling them inside the house where Rosie, pink-cheeked and tousled, awaited.

'Mum,' she said quickly, 'I've been meaning to tell you –'

'We're pregnant!' cried Niko. 'Let the world know!' He went to the kitchen window, opened it with a flourish and called out, 'We're pregnant! Ta-da! Preg-nant!'

'He's excited,' said Rosie. The semblance of a smile. 'Super excited,' she said.

'As are we all,' said Henry fluently, but Tillie could see that her father was also nervous. He has a vision, she thought, for how this must play out –

As do I.

Carefully they sat in the lounge room while Niko busied himself with coffee and homemade shortbread. Susan fidgeted with her bag. She said to Rosie, 'When are you –'

'October.'

'Not so big –'

'Loose clothes. I'm fine. Everything's fine.'

'Of course.' Susan put down her bag and said vaguely, 'October is the same month as my commission.'

'Uh-huh.'

Henry's voice, cutting through. 'Rosie?'

'Yes.' She blew out a long sigh. 'Mum,' she said, 'sorry I didn't tell you earlier.'

'It's okay,' said Susan quickly. 'Perfectly fine. Very happy for you both.'

But as her head sank beneath the weight of held-back tears, Rosie's utterance, though faint, was still audible.

'For God's sake.'

No more, thought Tillie. No more pretence and stepping-around. Remember George what's-his-name, *knowledge of what is possible* … She reached into her backpack and pulled out the leather-clad book.

'Rosie? Here's your diary.'

Susan glanced up. Rosie took the book, held it tight to her chest.

'Thanks,' she said. 'Hope it helped.'

'It did,' said Tillie, 'except for one thing. It's unfinished.'

Silence, broken after a moment by Niko's low whistling in the kitchen.

'It's a diary,' said Rosie, her voice a defensive croak. 'You don't *finish* diaries. You write for a while then stop when you can't be bothered.'

No more of this.

Tillie said to them all, 'Listen, please. I need to say something.'

Henry said, 'Tillie –'

'No, Dad. Listen.' Utterly determined now, she ploughed on. 'I was sad. To stop being sad, I had to find out about happiness. I asked you all to help me and you did.'

She paused, trying to slow her breathing.

'Niko showed me the importance of family and history. Mum told me about being able to accept who you are, bad parts as well as good. Rosie let me read her diary so I could see how people need to let go of the past and look to a brighter future. Dad told me that happiness is about being truthful, and vice versa.'

She waited for the right words.

'But none of you,' she said, 'does those things. None of you does what you say.'

Because it had come to this, the simplest equation; how could *she* be happy if those closest to her chose unhappiness for themselves?

She said, 'If family is so important, why are we never together? If it's necessary to accept who you are and let go of the past, why do my mother and sister behave as if they can't be in the same room? If happiness is really about truth, why do we have these family secrets that have never been resolved?'

The room was very still. Tillie was aware of Niko's renewed presence.

Henry spoke first. 'Tillie,' he said, 'you're right and I'm sorry, so very sorry –'

'It's my fault,' sniffed Susan, 'all mine –'

'No,' said Rosie, 'at my age, I should be able –'

The babble, the jangle, balcony-girl falling and flying, the cold windy desert –

'Stop it!' Tillie cried. 'Stop! I don't care who's to blame! I just want it finished!' She gripped her hands into fists, raised them to her face and said, 'It's not just me … I want all of us to be happy.'

Birthday Party Memory.

Rosie didn't fall.

But what –

What?

I pushed her, Susan admitted. Pushed my own child into a glass door. Hurt her for all time.

Pushed her?

Yes.

Why?

Angry, said Susan. Bitterly disappointed with myself as a mother and wife. As an artist. Locked into something I couldn't manage.

Locked into –

Tillie, she said, Rosie, there's no easy way … I hid it, I denied it, but the truth. Oh, God, the truth.

Mum?

Susan said, I'm an alcoholic.

That a word could be that way, as cold and black and heavy as a stone.

I don't any more, she said, I can't – but if I ever went back –

My fault too, Henry interjected. I knew, of course I did, but head in the sand, typical, I thought it would go away. She'll get better and then, then –

Wasn't coping, said Susan. Rosie was –

What?

Like me. Too much like me. Spirited. Born for the openness, the wilderness. It didn't seem possible that one child could contain so much life, but she did. And like me, she wouldn't take no … Rosie, I loved you very much but I couldn't cope with you, then I damaged you because I was drunk and angry. It was your birthday, you said something about a gift, I thought that's ungrateful, how dare you, I reached out and I pushed and –

Oh, God. I thought I'd killed you. Oh, God.

In the hospital –

They asked and I was going to admit it. I thought now's the time, tell the truth, but Henry whispered to me –

I told them that she tripped and fell.

Why?

My responsibility, he said, to fix this. I was the father, the protector who had failed to protect. Like my own father – unlike him, I was going to deal with it but I did it the wrong way. She fell, I said, she tripped on a toy and fell. Little Rosie, lying there, bound up – they asked again, when she could talk and Rosie, you –

I told them that I tripped and fell.

Yes. Yes, you did. Maybe you believed me, maybe not. I've never known, or asked. Head in the sand, thought it would all go away –

You came home, said Susan, with your bruising and your stitches and your poor little twisted eye, and I couldn't look at you because every time I did I was looking at my weakness, my stupidity – I couldn't, so I retreated. I thought there's no point. I'm no mother, I can't ever be a mother, so I retreated –

We both did.

Me to my art and Henry to whatever he was doing and that was how we lived, without proper acknowledgement of our damaged girl. Then Tillie came along and I'd stopped drinking so I thought, maybe I can be better this time, maybe I can love this little one without –

What? Mum?

Without hurting her. Without scarring her for life.

Susan stared at Rosie's hands, cupped over the sacredness of her stomach. Henry had gone to the verandah with Niko, the two men absorbing the span of the country that stretched before them as if that clean light and air might refresh all that had passed in this place, over time. Susan joined them, silently.

The coffee and shortbread sat untouched on a table. Tillie said, 'Rosie, Mum has a new work under way. It's about the connections between water and land and people, and it's massive, so she needs lots of space.'

Rosie's eyes were wet and blank.

'Mum could come here,' said Tillie. 'The barn could be her studio.'

Because then she could be with you, help you – help herself. Heal herself.

Make all of us happy.

Tillie and Rosie stood together in the late coppery sunshine. Further down, near the fence line, they could see Henry and Susan walking with Niko as he outlined the future: a couple of cows, more chickens, a piggery perhaps, definitely an expanded vegetable plot so they could sell at the Rocklea markets. He waved his arms enthusiastically; Niko, driven by the unquenchable spirit of an elder from the island of Naxos.

'Hey, MooMoo.'

'Hey, Rosie.'

'Are you cold? I can lend you my famous inside-out jacket.'

'I'm not cold.'

Henry and Niko straddling the fence like end-of-the-day yarning cowboys; Susan taking in the shifting hues and purple moods of the range. Rosie said, 'You did a good thing today.'

'I would've asked –'

'And I would've said no. Much better, this way.'

'Hope so.'

'Know so. MooMoo, give me your hand.'

'Why?'

'Just do it, Doofus. Okay. Top half of my belly. Feel that?'

'Yes.'

'How is it?'

'Really warm.'

Other words too, like powerful, glorious. Alive.

'You know what that is?'

'Your baby.'

'Ours,' said Rosie.

Early in October they drove to the waterfront park in Manly. Susan was quickly claimed by men and women in matching suits and escorted to a low stage that featured a line of plastic chairs and a podium. Her sculpture, completed the week before and trucked down to the park, had been fixed in place and covered with a satiny blue cloth that rippled in the breeze.

Tillie looked over the shredded, silvery water to the Port of Brisbane, hazed by heat and distance. Somewhere between the horizon and a wall of mangroves, a herd of long-necked cranes and derricks walked in the same direction. Like vigilant animals, she thought, patrolling the world's perimeter.

Strange but comforting.

She heard a burst of amplified music and turned to see that a small crowd had assembled in front of the stage. Henry said, 'We're family, we have reserved seats. Front row.'

They sat beneath an awning and waited, Tillie trying without success to catch her mother's eye and wave. A nervous Henry rubbed his hands up and down his trousers. Eventually Snake – wearing a collared shirt, Tillie realised, he never did that! – said in a chatty kind of way, 'How's the book going, Mr Bassett?'

'Pardon, Felix?'

'I was telling him.' Tillie blushed.

'Okay,' said Henry, 'the Book of Bond. Actually, I've abandoned that particular idea.'

Tillie looked at her father; his long ears and nose, bushy brows, the coarse tufts of grey that peeked out from the vee at the top of his shirt. She wanted to hug him.

'A bit silly, really,' mused Henry, 'and no doubt a waste of time. So, yes, abandoned and moved on. Rosie's partner – Niko, you've met him? – Niko needed some help on his farm. I've become a gardener, haven't I, Tillie?'

He had too; on their frequent visits she'd watched him hoeing and planting, patting down the soil, spraying, watering, his slow but somehow elegant precision now applied to the nurture of plants.

Henry said, 'There's a great deal of satisfaction to be gained from growing things.'

Polite applause lifted their eyes to the podium where Susan stood behind a florid man in a grey suit. He was leaning into the microphone, introducing her.

'… an artist whose unique insight …'

Tillie leaned forward – to a trill, a ringtone.

'Oops,' said Henry. He reached into his pocket and retrieved his phone, was about to switch to silent when he saw the caller ID.

'Might just take this …'

He hunched down, pressed the phone, listened and whispered. Back at the podium, Tillie saw that her mother had reached the microphone. As she spoke, Susan used one hand to pin down her notes and the other to restrain her hair, which was threatening to flee with each gust of the strengthening breeze.

'… particularly like to thank the council for their faith …'

Henry said urgently, 'We have to go!'

'Dad, we can't. Mum's talking –'

But already he was bounding towards the stage, as long-legged and urgent as an emu. People muttered and scowled; Henry's voice came in snatches and grabs.

'Susan, it's happening … she's early … Susan, now!'

'Oh, wow,' said Snake. He gripped Tillie's hand.

Susan almost ate the microphone. 'I have to go,' she said loudly. 'My daughter is having a baby!' She wobbled away from the podium before kicking off her stilettos, giving them to the startled-looking man in the grey suit and clambering barefoot down a set of steps to Henry's outstretched hands.

'Come on –'

'Wait,' said Susan.

'No, we can't –'

She ran across to the sculpture, tugged at a cord and released the binds on the cloth. The blue satin rose before slipping and going lopsided. Snake darted away from his seat, grabbed the other side of the cloth, straightened it and lifted exultantly. As wind filled the fabric and blew the cloth into the sky, people applauded spontaneously – and laughed when the blueness overturned and snagged on a tree like a scrap of fallen sky.

But the sculpture was exposed. The crowd saw circles and curves and arcs. They saw a structure that had been carefully designed to look carefree. They looked for details and saw waves and rolling winds and contradictions; the long caress, long burn of the sun. They saw dunes that might never end, sea-worn rocks and caves, air, grit, light and shadow, and in seeing all this they sensed the single wonderment of existence: that any being might defeat the odds in order to survive, adapt and eventually prosper.

More applause … The crowd watched a small child waddle across to the sculpture and climb through a circle, tumble to the other side before righting herself and bobbing up with a watermelon smile. As if released, more children –

'Come on!' said Henry.

For once, he drove fast.

'He's perfect,' said Snake. He sounded bewildered.

'Yes, he is.' Rosie touched Snake's hand. She said, 'We know how lucky we are.'

Susan, stroking the sole of a tiny foot, asked, 'What will you call him?'

Rosie kissed the baby's pink brow. 'Alexander,' she said.

'After my grandfather,' Nikos told them proudly. 'His name was Alexandros. It means defender of the people.'

'This robust little bloke,' said Henry, 'looks like he could well become a defender of the people.'

'No pressure,' admonished Susan. 'He might be an artist.'

'Or we might let him find his own way,' said Rosie. 'Hey, little one. Find your own way?' She nuzzled and soothed, nuzzled some more. When Tillie asked if she could, just for a moment, have a hold, Rosie was happy to oblige. Happy too when her mother took Alexander, welcomed him and wept gently on to the baby's fontanelle.

Near their house the jacarandas were in full flower, their spheres of mauve spilling along the streets like bowling balls. Snake had been dropped home, having been granted permission to come over for dinner, and her parents had gone straight inside for a cuppa – 'We're getting old,' said Susan, Henry adding, 'We grandparents need our renewal.'

Tillie stood alone. She knew it now, had known for a while, that happiness in a pure sense does not exist. It might be a texture or a brightness, a murmur, a reflection from a sculpture or the opening cry of a newborn – but it comes and goes like light, like the breeze. Suspension … we are never utterly happy or utterly sad, never utterly anything but many things, at once, for as long as our grace is provided.

We are the swoop of a bird and the crawl of a lizard.

We are the morning chill and the noontime bake.

We are variegated patterns of sunshine and shadow.

We are the rising scent of grass, of blood, of river water.

We are ant and elephant.

We are city and land, desert and shore.

We are thunder and dew, the mystery and the evidence.

We are one person, she had realised, and many more besides.

We are alive and part of the great continuance, and that is enough. That is all.

That night, as her father showed her Boyfriend and Best Friend with Mended Wondrous Heart how to make lasagne, as her mother allowed herself to dream of what might be and her sister gazed with love at the faces of the two people who would carry her forward, Tillie Bassett sat in the garden. She smelled the subtlety of flowers, listened to the cars and kitchen clatter, and she watched the sky, forever darkening and lightening. When she heard a bird whistle the beginnings of sleep, Tillie thought to return to the house. Soon the family would eat, but first she wanted to be with her mother for their nightly ritual, to review their todays and plan their tomorrows. It was, thought Tillie, a simple but worthwhile pleasure; as much as anyone need do.